THE
TOP 10
MISTAKES

I MADE MY
FIRST YEAR
AS A
COPYWRITER

THE
TOP 10
MISTAKES
I MADE MY
FIRST YEAR
AS A
COPYWRITER

How I Tripped, Stumbled, and
Finally Found My Footing in
the World of Copywriting

ANN SCHREIBER

FOX
POINTE
PUBLISHING

This book is a memoir. It contains the author's present memories of experiences over time. Some names may have been changed, some events may have been condensed, and some dialogue may have been recreated.

www.foxpointepublishing.com/author-ann-schreiber

Library of Congress Cataloging-in-Publication Data
Schreiber, Ann, author.
Town, Scotty, designer.
The Top 10 Mistakes I Made My First Year as a Copywriter / Ann Schreiber. – First edition.
Summary: The author shares hard-earned knowledge in copywriting and self-employment with readers.
ISBN: 978-1-955743-08-2 (softcover)
[1. Freelance & Self-Employment – Business & Economics. 2. Success – Self-Help.
3. Memoirs – Biography & Autobiography.]
Library of Congress Control Number: 2 0 2 4 9 5 3 0 5 6

Printed and bound in the United States of America
First printing in March 2025

A NOTE TO MY READERS

IF YOU ARE READING THIS PAGE, THANK YOU. It means that you have decided to take a chance on me or you are one of my family members or friends who bought this book to support me and help me get some reviews on Goodreads and Amazon. While I thank the latter group for always being there for me, I'll thank them in more detail at the end of this book.

For now, I want to focus on those of you who decided to purchase this book by choice. It's those of you—whether you are an aspiring copywriter, a college student studying content marketing, or someone stuck in a rut with a content business that isn't growing—thank you.

Thank you for buying my book, for taking this chance, and for trusting me with your time and money.

Am I an expert on the topic of copywriting? Am I the end-all-be-all when writing great content for websites? Absolutely not. But, I'll tell you this—these last two years since I officially started my business have been quite the wild ride. And I'm good at what I do.

I've been far more successful than I could ever have imagined. As I look to wrap up my second official year in March 2025, about the time this book will be coming out, I'll have a lot to celebrate.

I've expanded my business outside of Upwork. Yes, I am still a huge fan of Upwork, which generates many new leads for me whenever I need them. But I've grown and don't need to rely on that platform exclusively to help my business grow. Clients are finding me outside the platform, and it's been amazing.

I published my first book, *Perseverance. Reinvention.* Initially, I went the self-publishing route and released the book in June 2024. Since then, a publisher has picked up that book, and it is in its second release. Thank you, Fox Pointe Publishing, for recognizing my talent and agreeing that I have something to share with others.

If you're reading this, I've published my second book, too. And that means I have achieved one of my life goals—to help others develop their love for writing and turn it into a profitable business. Okay, maybe I'm getting ahead of myself here. So let's just say this—I've reached a point where I have something to share with others. I've taken the long road and learned many things about what not to do when starting a small business, especially one focused on writing.

So that brings us to now and why this book even exists in the first place. As you'll see from the chapters to come, I pretty much jumped into my business overnight. I had been doing the freelance thing as a side gig for several years. But, when an unanticipated career change occurred in January of 2023, I found myself in a unique position.

Do I keep doing just some of what I love for somebody else, taking orders, and finding my energy depleted at the end of each day? Or do I take that chance on myself, jumping in with both feet and all my clothes on, learning how to sink or swim? Thankfully, I took lifeguarding courses as a teenager and was able to save myself. But, perhaps more importantly, I embraced the opportunity to finally do what I love to do each and every day. Yes, I made some mistakes, which is the purpose of this book. Those mistakes made me stronger, wiser, and a better solo entrepreneur and business owner than I ever could have managed for myself.

Am I a millionaire? No. That's not my goal.

I make a comfortable, more than modest living. But most importantly, I end my day with a smile. When I lay my head on the pillow at night, I know I spent my time doing something I love during the day. Even better? I got paid to do it.

I want to share what I learned in my first two years as a copywriter in this book. Yes, I know the title says first year. And the truth is, I learned most of this in that first year, but it has taken me until now, about the time of this book's release, to reconcile all of those mistakes and turn my business into a well-oiled machine.

The happy reality is that there is plenty of work out there for all of us. Great content is in demand. Consumers want readily available information to answer their questions and solve any challenge. As writers, we can help do just that.

Why reinvent the wheel and make the same mistakes that I did when you can skip right over all of that?

So again, here we are. Thank you for being here, for reading, and for paying attention to what I have to say. The words in this book will save you time, money, and headaches so that you can start doing what you love because that's what I get to do. I want that for you, too.

As one of my colleagues once said to me, she writes words for websites. And that's what I do today, too. And this book? It's designed to help you get all that business and back-office stuff squared away so you can do the same.

If you love to write and want to make money doing it, but you're not sure where to start because you're afraid of making some mistakes, this book is for you.

TABLE OF CONTENTS

Why I Became a Writer 1

What is this Book Really About? 11

Mistake #1: Going Cheap and Getting a Poorly Designed Website 15

Mistake #2: Not Having Clients Sign a Statement of Work 27

Mistake #3: Missteps in Pricing–The Cost of Undervaluing My Services 41

Mistake #4: Not Spending Enough Time on Lead Generation for Copywriters ... 53

Mistake #5: Not Looking Out for My Business with Business Liability Insurance ... 65

Mistake #6: Waiting Too Long to Leverage the Potential of Social Media 77

Mistake #7: Not Posting Regular Content to My Blog 89

Mistake #8: Relying Too Much (or Not Enough) on Artificial Intelligence 103

Mistake #9: Failing to Develop Business Partnerships 117

Mistake #10: Not Starting My Business Sooner 131

Lessons Learned: Turning Mistakes into Mastery 145

Mistakes Are Proof That You are Trying 159

Looking Forward: My Second Year (and Beyond) as a Copywriter 173

Acknowledgments 186

Glossary of Terms 189

WHY I BECAME A WRITER

I'LL BE HONEST, I LOVE TELLING MY STORY. No, I'm not trying to be vain. It's just that I think I'm one of the lucky ones. I have a career that I love. I get to write words for websites and support my clients in their efforts to drive more consumers to their websites. For me, that's a pretty awesome proposition.

And while I just officially started my copywriting business in March of 2023, I've been writing for far longer than that. In fact, my earliest memories are around age seven. For those of you who don't know me, you can pick that jaw up off the floor. I'm not that old. But yes, I have over 40 years of experience as a writer. Whether I am writing for myself or others, this has been ingrained in me for a long time.

So, where did it all begin? And why am I telling you all of this? I guess its because I don't want you to think that I just woke up one morning thinking I wanted to be a writer and had the skills to do it. The path to get here was a long and winding road. And while it took me a long time to get to the point where I am now, the journey has been well worth it.

Like I said, my memories of writing go back to when I was honing my reading skills. I had been an early reader, often held back in class to wait for other kids to catch up. So what else could I do with my time other than to take that vocabulary I was learning with my reading and turn it into storytelling. I would pen stories on pieces of construction paper, and later in small notebooks that my mom had given to me.

I was able to further develop my writing skills in middle school when I wrote for the school newspaper and the yearbook. I learned the art of interviewing and digging for information. I learned the art of listening and giving the speaker a bit of time to explain their answer in further detail before jumping in with the next question.

In high school, I jumped into the school paper once again. I started as a reporter during my freshman year and then took on editing positions over my sophomore and junior year. By my senior year, I was the editor-in-chief of the paper. It was during that time that I decided I wanted to attend journalism school. But I didn't have money set aside for college, so heading off to a four-year school right from the get-go just wasn't in the cards.

Instead, I spent my senior year taking college courses. By the time I graduated from high school, I was already a sophomore at the local junior college. I served as co-editor-in-chief of the local junior college newspaper for my sophomore year. Then it was time to transfer to the University of Minnesota.

I was accepted into journalism school and started taking journalism courses. But an unfortunate turn of events happened when the university faced a loss of their journalism school accreditation. And it was about that time that our class was studying the anticipated salary that would come with an entry-level position at a local newspaper. I'll just say this: it wasn't much.

I decided to change paths, switching to an English degree. Ultimately, this turned out to be the best possible decision. I had the opportunity to study creative writing, technical writing, and storytelling—my courses covered everything from classic literature to modern communication theories, each teaching me new ways to connect with different audiences.

The creative writing classes were especially helpful, teaching how to stir emotions and paint pictures with words. At the same time, the technical writing classes improved my ability to explain complex ideas simply and clearly. This skill became super important for me later on as a content writer, particularly when I started working with tech startups where I needed to break down tech-speak for everyday users. Though, I have to admit, tech writing gives me the least amount of energy today.

My communications courses taught me about the power of media and how people perceive messages. I learned how to analyze audiences and craft my writing to fit specific needs, which aided in growing my ability to persuade and inform—and that's what copywriting is all about. These skills have been fundamental in my career, helping me adjust my writing style for various clients and industry needs.

My experiences at university built a strong foundation for the work I do today. But, as it turned out, my career would venture off in new directions for the next two decades, teaching me other skills that were less writing-focused, but fundamental for the future business I would build.

I won't bore you with the details of those next twenty years. The short story is that my career took me to places I never could have imagined, literally and figuratively. I took on various sales and marketing leadership roles, learning all about the marketing space and how content marketing—in my case content writing—fit into the broader world of advertising and creating brand awareness.

In those early years in the marketing space, I also attended the University of St. Thomas in Minneapolis, earning my graduate degree in business communications. Basically, that's a fancy way of saying marketing. Business communications is about how companies talk to their customers, their employees, and the rest of the world. It's like the backbone of marketing, where everything you say and how you say it can either make or break your connection with your audience.

And I'd be remiss to leave out that this was where I learned about the 4Ps of marketing. Those in the marketing space know that these are the core of any marketing strategy, and they line up perfectly with content writing and copywriting. For those of you unfamiliar, here's a quick crash course.

- **Product:** When I write, the product isn't just the article or blog post; it's the idea or message that's being delivered. It's what grabs the reader's attention.

- **Price:** This isn't always about money. It's about the effort the reader has to put in to understand the content. My job is to make it as easy as possible for them.

- **Place:** It's all about where the content shows up. Could be a website, a blog, or a social media post. It has to be right where the audience can find it.

- **Promotion:** This is where the fun happens. It's about getting people to see the content. Using the right words to make the message pop and share it in a way that makes people want to read and engage.

Understanding these concepts helped me see the bigger picture of how my writing fits into marketing campaigns and business strategies. And as we know, it's not just about crafting words; it's about crafting messages that meet business goals and connect deeply with people.

Now back to the chronology of events that brings us to today. After earning my master's degree in 2007, I continued on in those sales and marketing roles. Some of those positions gave me the opportunity to travel the world—Mexico, Bulgaria, Colombia, Canada, the Philippines, India, and more. And while these roles weren't specific to writing and I desperately wished for a way to steer my role back to focus on writing, it simply wasn't going to happen.

Then, in 2017, while working for a large, global business process management organization, I was introduced to the Upwork platform. You'll hear me say multiple times in this book that I am a big fan of Upwork. At the time, I was the head of corporate marketing and, while I was able to spend some of my time doing business writing, the other priorities and demands of the role kept me from staying on top of the content-related work. Upwork allowed me the opportunity to connect with other writers to help augment the work I just couldn't manage on my own.

I recall making a joke to some of my colleagues outside the organization that if things ever changed in my career and time was on my side, I would create my own Upwork profile and seize the opportunity to take on some freelance writing work. After all, the experience of hiring candidates from those early days on the platform would make it easier for me to sell my services on the freelancing side of the business.

That opportunity presented itself far sooner than I expected. In October 2018, I made a job change, walking away from a lucrative well-paying position for the opportunity to go back into commissioned sales. By May 2019, it was clear that the position wasn't a good fit, and the only way to make it a good fit was to relocate to Los Angeles. For reasons I discuss in my previous book, that wasn't an option. So I took a severance package.

I took the opportunity to familiarize myself with the Upwork platform as a freelancer rather than a client. I found the tool easy to use, and, within just a couple of days, I had my first client. Before long, I had a steady stream of clients and I was generating a decent side hustle income aside from that little parachute I had received at the end of my last job, giving me something fun to do between applying for new positions.

When I landed a full-time job again just a couple of months later, I decided to keep the freelance gig going. Over the years, I had the ability to refine my writing skills, master writing for search engine optimization (SEO), and learned how to juggle multiple clients while also managing the responsibilities of my full-time job commitments.

Fast-forward to January 2023. Though the writing was on the wall, I was surprised to find my role eliminated after the holidays. While I allowed myself to grieve and shed a few tears, I found that I didn't have time to wallow in the concerns associated with unemployment. I was engaged to be married just one month later; my second marriage and one that I had no intentions to begin on the wrong foot.

So I did three things: I reached out to my connections, networked the heck out of LinkedIn, and submitted application after application. Over the course of two weeks, I had numerous interviews. Unfortunately, they all seemed to end with a common theme. I heard that my skills were out of date, my salary expectations were too high, and my recent titles were too senior. Honestly, it felt like I was being told I was too old without being told I was too old. It was frustrating, and a bit annoying, to say the least.

But there is a silver lining here, because when I wasn't busy sending off my resume, scheduling interviews and coffee chats, I was also reaching out to those clients that I had been working with throughout the last several years. I even reached out to some that I had had to "let go" because their content needs were too much for me to manage on top of getting through a divorce, getting my youngest child through an illness, high school, and college, and keeping up with full-time employment.

To my surprise, when I asked those clients if they had more work to send my way, they all responded with not only "yes," but, in some cases, a comment to the effect of, "we've just been waiting for you." Before I knew it, I had a steady stream of work and had offset about 60% of the income I had been making from that full-time position.

With a few weeks of a severance package remaining, and only a 40% gap to not just meet but exceed my previous income, the next step became clear—it was time to turn this side hustle into a full-time gig.

But there were two potential obstacles. The first was about benefits. At the time, I didn't realize that buying into a self-employment benefit plan was so easy. I feared that I wouldn't have benefits as a full-time freelancer. And I also worried that my then-fiancé (now-husband) wouldn't feel so great about marrying someone who had been gainfully employed and was suddenly venturing into the gig-economy.

Thankfully, I didn't have much to worry about. He asked me a few questions as devil's advocate, to which I had an answer for each one. He told me that he'd add me to his benefits plan after the wedding.

And the rest is history—kind of—because what happens next is really what the bulk of this book is about. It's about growing a business. It's about embracing a passion for what I love to do—write. And it's about persevering as a solo entrepreneur, small business owner, and female-owned business.

So, I know that was a rather long-winded way of setting myself up to answer the question that this chapter is intended to be about. And that is—why did I become a writer?

The answer is simple. When I write, I feel more like myself than at any other time of the day. I have the opportunity to express myself, even when I am not writing about my own opinions or views. I have the opportunity to learn and grow.

Writing ignites a special kind of joy for me. While my business is named Copywriting For You, most of my days are spent content writing. This means I spend my time writing blogs, articles, and landing pages for companies all over the U.S. and, sometimes, across the globe. The goal? To inform. Every piece is a chance to enrich someone's understanding or answer their questions, and that's a big part of what drives me.

There's a distinct thrill in researching a new topic. I get to put on my detective hat, dig through information, and piece together something both insightful and engaging. The process of crafting a narrative or laying out facts is like solving a puzzle—and these puzzles I am actually good at. When I finally send off a completed piece to a client, the sense of accomplishment is unbeatable. It's like handing over a part of me that I've polished and perfected.

But I need to spend a bit of time here making sure we're all aligned on copywriting and content writing. While often used interchangeably, these are two unique forms of writing that serve unique purposes. Copywriting is all about persuasion—think ads and promotional materials designed to drive action and result in a conversion or sale. Content writing, on the other hand, leans towards educating and engaging the audience through a more narrative style. My days are mostly filled with the latter, and I love it for the depth it allows me to explore.

Every day as a writer makes me sharper. Each week, a new inquiry from a prospective client opens up a world I've yet to explore. This is not just a job; it's a journey of continuous learning and improvement. It's empowering to know that with every assignment I'm not only helping a client but also expanding my own horizons and where I'll be able to take my business in the future.

I cherish the unpredictability—never knowing exactly what challenge will pop up next. But one thing remains constant: the love for what I do. Every morning, I wake up excited to see what the day holds, ready to tackle whatever writing task comes my way. This isn't just work; it's a passion that fulfills and defines me.

Yes, that's why I became a writer. I truly believe it was what I was born to do. And how cool is it that I can help businesses grow while doing what I love?

WHAT IS THIS BOOK
REALLY ABOUT?

NOW WE'VE COME TO THE SECTION that you've been waiting for—those ten mistakes I made during my first year as a copywriter. I promise, we're almost there. But I want to clear something up. These are by far and away not the only mistakes I made during my first year as a business owner in the content world. The truth is that I continue to make mistakes each and every day. Some are big. Some are small.

These ten that I decided to share in this book are the doozies. Even if you take notes from my woes and build processes to avoid these same mistakes, please know that you'll make more—lots of them. And that's not always a bad thing.

I get it. Making mistakes is the last thing you want to do, especially when starting out. But here's the thing—they're not just inevitable; they're incredibly valuable. Every slip-up, big or small, is a chance to learn something new. And yes, while some mistakes can feel like a real facepalm moment, they often provide the juiciest, low-hanging fruit for growth.

Let's talk about those small mistakes first. These little blunders? They're golden. They help you fine-tune your process, figure out what works and what doesn't, and sometimes guide you to discover your niche. That's right, messing up a bit here and there can help you zoom in on the exact area you excel in, or sometimes, they push you to cast a wider net.

When I first dipped my toes into writing professionally, I started with personal finance because of my employment background with big names like FICO and Experian. It was comfortable. But I might have never ventured beyond that comfort zone if I hadn't made some bold moves (and a few missteps along the way). Mistakes pushed me to take risks, try new things, and, eventually, broaden my horizons.

Let me share an example. A couple of years ago, I took on a new client who found me on Upwork. His company was in the personalized marketing space. Their platform used machine learning to generate personalized recommendations. Think of a retailer who might use a platform to recommend certain shoes and accessories at the point of purchase when you add a pair of designer jeans to your cart.

I totally understand the space, and I have experience in it. But I'm not good at writing about it, and it totally drained me. Was it a mistake to take on the client? Yes and no. But was it a mistake to part ways? Not at all. It wasn't the right fit, and now I know.

That said, while that particular niche was not right for me, I'm not just a personal finance writer today. I've branched out into health and wellness, dental, parenting, technology, pet care, home construction, leadership development, and even academic writing. I've written about romance and relationships—an excellent fit for someone getting back in the dating game in her mid-40s.

Each new area has been a step into the unknown, a place where mistakes were waiting to happen. And happen they did. But with each mistake, I learned a bit more about that industry, about my writing style, and about what my readers wanted. And I had a golden opportunity—to continue on with the topics and industries I loved writing in, and to part ways with those I didn't.

So don't hold back because you are afraid you might screw up now and again. Embrace the mistakes, learn from them, and use them to carve out your unique path in the content writing world. Remember, spilled milk isn't something to cry over—it's just another opportunity to clean up, learn, and grow. Each day is a new chance to get better, believe me. The wide range of topics I now tackle confidently all started with the willingness to mess up and learn from each and every stumble along the way.

Alright, let's buckle up and get into the meat of this book—the ten big doozies, the mishaps, the "what was I thinking?" moments from my first year as a copywriter. We're about to unpack a suitcase full of "oops" moments that taught me more than any success ever could.

- **Going Cheap and Getting a Poorly Designed Website:** Ever tried to save a buck and ended up paying ten? Yeah, me too.

- **Not Having Clients Sign a Statement of Work:** Let's just say, verbal agreements are as sturdy as a house of cards in a windstorm.

- **Missteps in Pricing—The Cost of Undervaluing My Services:** Spoiler alert: Selling yourself short isn't a bargain sale; it's just short-selling yourself.

- **Not Spending Enough Time on Lead Generation for Copywriters:** Because hoping the phone rings isn't a marketing strategy.

- **Not Looking Out for My Business with Business Liability Insurance:** Turns out, 'it won't happen to me' is not a great insurance policy.

- **Waiting Too Long to Leverage the Potential of Social Media:** Late to the social media party, and no, fashionably late doesn't count here.

- **Not Posting Regular Content to My Blog:** Who knew that 'build it and they will come' doesn't apply to blogs?

- **Relying Too Much (or Not Enough) on Artificial Intelligence:** Finding the AI sweet spot is harder than it sounds.

- **Failing to Develop Business Partnerships:** Lone wolfing it might be cool in movies, but not so much in business.

- **Not Starting My Business Sooner:** The classic 'coulda, woulda, shoulda'.

As we roll through these chapters, you'll see how each blunder, each moment where I wanted to smack my head against the wall—a soft wall, but a wall nonetheless—was actually a stepping stone to something better. So, don't sweat the small stuff, and even the big stuff—because, in the grand scheme of things, it's all just stuff. Let's learn, laugh a bit at my past self, and maybe (just maybe) help you sidestep some of these oopsies.

MISTAKE #1
GOING CHEAP AND GETTING
A POORLY DESIGNED WEBSITE

AS YOU KNOW BY NOW, in January 2023, I finally made the decision I should have made years ago. I decided to remove myself from the corporate world and pursue a career as a full-time freelance content writer and copywriter. While I have been writing since I was very young, it just never seemed that doing this full-time was in the cards. But eventually, the stars aligned. By March 2023, I had established an S-Corp, and my business—Copywriting For You—was born.

I was wildly successful right from the get-go and, even today, I am blessed to have a steady stream of new clients and a reliable set of long-term clients who have been with me before I became official. But if I said that all of that behind-the-scenes stuff was easy, I'd be lying. There was far more to it than I realized.

I made many mistakes in my first year. I made so many mistakes that I feel like I'd be doing a disservice to all future content writers looking to start their own businesses if I didn't share what I've learned along the way. And so to start, we absolutely need to talk about your small business website.

DON'T UNDERESTIMATE THE VALUE OF A GREAT WEBSITE

Here's the thing—when I got started and set up my legal structure, I assumed I would just take in work through Upwork and call it a day. And the fact is I could have done that and could still do that. Upwork has been, and continues to be, an amazing source of amazing clients. But word started getting around, and I had people reaching out to me outside of Upwork who didn't want to join the platform and send me contracts that way.

This got me thinking—I need a website, right? RIGHT! Anyone running a business these days needs a great website. If you want people to find you, you need that online presence. So, I hired the first contractor who gave me the lowest bid. Yes, I found his company on Upwork.

But in this case, hiring him was not Upwork's fault. It was mine and mine alone. I sourced the work to the lowest bidder, investing just a few hundred dollars on a very rudimentary website. And it showed.

Here are all the things that were wrong about it:

- Poor, amateur-looking, design
- Crazy slow load times that frustrated visitors
- Poor navigation that made finding information difficult
- Lack of compelling imagery to capture interest
- No video content to engage users
- A sitemap that did absolutely no good
- Unprofessional fonts and mismatched colors
- Broken links that led to nowhere

THE PROFESSIONAL EMBARRASSMENT OF A POORLY DESIGNED WEBSITE

So, this begs the question—why was my website so important to me? If clients found me through LinkedIn, word-of-mouth, and networking, wasn't that enough? Well, sure, if I wanted to grow at a slow pace. The truth is that the world of freelancing is a constant hustle. Clients can come and go. Even long-term clients sometimes have a change of strategy and may need more or less content, which can create income fluctuations.

A website was a means to the end, or perhaps the means to the beginning. If I wanted to increase my lead pipeline, I needed to ensure prospective clients could find me their way. And with people spending 6 ½ hours or more online every day, I needed that website. But what happened when they found my website was the problem.

Having a website just wasn't enough. That poor website design painted a pretty awful picture. I worried it would leave those prospective clients wondering about wanting to work with me. Why? A bad website is bound to make them have the following thoughts:

- Doubts about my professionalism

- Concerns about the quality of my work

- Hesitation to trust my services

- Assumptions that I'm not serious about my business

- Fear that I lack attention to detail

- The perception that I'm outdated or out of touch

- Worries about my reliability and commitment

- Reluctance to refer me to others

And this was the last thing I wanted as a new business owner who had turned her side hustle into a full-time gig.

DON'T MAKE MY MISTAKE: INVEST IN A QUALITY WEBSITE FROM THE GET-GO

My advice to all of you new writers? Go big or go home. If you can't afford a website, wait until you can—but do what you can to find the financial means to get one. A website is pretty much a non-negotiable in today's business world, and it is your best opportunity to strut your stuff and help develop a trusted relationship with those potential customers.

Here's the question—how much does a professional website cost? According to Forbes, a small business's website costs range from $2,000 to $9,000. And it's not a one-and-done endeavor. There are many recurring costs, from maintenance to site upgrades, plug-ins, and more. Those costs can easily run you about $1,200 a year. But I'll tell you this—it will cost you a lot more to fix a poorly designed website than to do it right the first time.

You can start your website in stages to manage cost. You can start with the bare bones and grow it from there—in fact, I'm very much in that phase now with my newly designed website. I'll surely add more in the months and years to come. But, if you ask my opinion—you asked, right?—I would tell you to start with the following six key pages:

HOMEPAGE

The homepage is the first impression visitors get of your business. It should convey who you are, what you do, and how you can help potential clients. Aim for around 500 words, ensuring it's well-organized and visually appealing. Include a strong headline, an engaging introduction, and easy navigation to other key pages.

This page helps with SEO by using relevant keywords and providing a clear structure that search engines can easily index. Interlinking to other pages like Services, About Us, and your blog makes navigating your site easy for visitors and search engines.

ABOUT US PAGE

The About Us page is where you build trust and show your brand's personality. Share your story, mission, and values to connect with visitors personally. Approximately 500 words will give you enough space to be detailed without overwhelming readers.

This page is important for SEO, too, as it allows you to include keywords related to your business and industry. It's also a great place to link to your Services and Contact Us pages, encouraging visitors to learn more about what you offer and how to get in touch.

SERVICES PAGE

Your Services page is where you outline what you offer and how it benefits your clients. Shoot for 500 words to detail each service, highlighting features, benefits, and why clients should choose you.

For example, my new services page clearly highlights the following services that I have to offer:

- Website content
- Blog content
- Article writing
- LinkedIn content

- Resumés

- Cover Letters

Detailed descriptions help search engines understand your offerings, making it easier for potential clients to find you. Interlink to relevant blog posts and your Contact Us page to guide visitors through decision-making and encourage them to reach out.

BLOG PAGE

If you are a content writer, you need a blog. Period. Regularly updated blog posts can target various keywords, keeping your site fresh and relevant in search engine rankings. Each blog post should be around 800-1000 words, depending on the topic, though I encourage some long-form content, too (2,000 words or more).

The blog page itself should introduce what your blog is about and link to individual posts. Interlinking between blog posts and other pages like Services and About Us helps visitors find related content and keeps them exploring your site. After all, you want them to spend more time on your website to learn about you and how you can help their business.

FAQ PAGE

You may disagree with me on this one, but I strongly believe in the importance of the FAQ page. I recommend one to all new clients who don't have one already. The FAQ page addresses potential clients' common questions and concerns and boosts your credibility. This page should be concise yet informative, with each question and answer pair being around 50-100 words.

By including keywords in your answers, you help improve SEO and provide quick, valuable information to visitors. Plus, why not save everyone some time by answering some important questions right off the bat?

CONTACT US PAGE

The Contact Us page is where potential clients go to get in touch with you. It should include a contact form, your email address, phone number, and links to your social media profiles such as LinkedIn, Facebook, X (formerly known as Twitter), Instagram, and Pinterest. Keep the text to around 300-500 words, ensuring it's straightforward and easy to understand.

This page is great for SEO as it provides location-based keywords, such as Copywriter in Woodbury, MN, and ensures search engines know how visitors can reach you. Interlinking to your About Us and Services pages can help visitors learn more before contacting you, making their overall experience smooth and informative.

Oh, and my new favorite addition to my Contact Us page is the Book a Call option, which takes visitors directly to my Calendly page. This allows them to conveniently schedule time with me to discuss a project, scope out a blog, and more.

THOSE VALUE-ADDS FOR A HIGH-QUALITY WEBSITE

You might think that the six pages I mentioned above are overkill for a new website. But if you are going to spend the money on a basic site, adding another page or two will likely not break the bank. And, trust me, you will want to add even more pages later.

I just added a Partners page to highlight the professional connections I can make for my clients. Later, I plan to add landing pages to dive deep into my service offerings. As I said before, your website is an itera-tive process, and you need to start somewhere. For me, having those six pages I mentioned above was non-negotiable.

A great small business website is about more than just having the right pages. It needs to be quality, with a capital Q. Here's what your website needs and what poorly constructed websites typically lack:

FAST PAGE LOAD SPEEDS

Nobody has time—or patience—to wait these days for a slow website to load. Ideally, your page load speeds should be under two seconds. Anything longer and you risk losing potential clients who will simply move on to a competitor. And trust me, plenty of other content writers or copywriters are happy to take your business.

Fast load times improve user experience and make your website more appealing. Search engines love quick-loading sites, so it helps you to get found more easily. Investing in good hosting and optimized images and scripts are key steps to ensure your site is lightning-fast.

HIGH-QUALITY IMAGERY

People are visual creatures, and high-quality images can make a huge difference in how your website is perceived. Blurry or generic stock photos won't cut it. Invest in professional photography and headshots regularly. If your budget doesn't allow this upfront, go for high-quality stock images representing your brand.

Great imagery can attract visitors, keep them engaged, and make your content more memorable. Remember, the right pictures can tell your story better than words alone, so don't skimp on this aspect.

VIDEO CONTENT

Video content is a fantastic way to engage your visitors and convey your message effectively. Whether it's a short introduction about your business, client testimonials, or how-to guides, videos can make your site more dynamic and interesting. And if 88% of marketers say that video is a big part of their marketing strategy, it should be part of yours, too.

Videos keep visitors on your site longer, leading to higher conversion rates. Adding videos to your site can give you a competitive edge, as more people consume video content daily.

However, I know that video content is expensive. During my second year of business, I invested about $3,000 in candid (and not-so-candid) shots and two videos to help promote my business. You can find them on my website at www.copywritingforyou.net. I started with a short promotional video and a two-minute brand story video, and I plan to make new videos every 12 to 18 months to further promote my copywriting and content writing business. Now I even create my own videos that I share on my YouTube page, my Facebook business page, and my Instagram. If you're an Instagrammer, be sure to follow me at @ write_read_write_repeat.

GREAT CONTENT

Content is king, as they say. Your website's content needs to be clear, engaging, and well-written. And if you are a copywriter, this should be no problem. It's about having informative text and using a tone that resonates with your audience. I like to write in a more conversational tone, almost like we're together chatting away. You might prefer a more formal approach. Or maybe you're a closet comedian, and your writing lets it all come out.

Whatever approach you take, high-quality content helps establish your authority in your field, builds trust with your visitors, and improves your SEO. Remember to keep your content fresh and updated regularly to keep people coming back and to maintain your search engine rankings. Shoot for a blog post on your new website at least once a week if you can. And yes, I know this is sometimes easier said than done.

MOBILE-FRIENDLY DESIGN

With 60.67% of web traffic from mobile devices, a mobile-friendly design is no longer optional. Your website needs to look and function just as well on smartphones and tablets as on desktops.

A responsive design helps your site adjust to different screen sizes and provides a better user experience regardless of the device. This makes your site more accessible to a wider audience and improves search engine rankings, as search engines prioritize mobile-friendly sites.

DON'T MAKE THE MISTAKE THAT I DID: SKIP OUT ON A POORLY DESIGNED WEBSITE

A website is what can help you grow your business in this internet-driven society. It's where consumers will go to learn about your products and services. So, getting it right the first time will be well worth the cost and will save you a lot of wasted dollars down the road.

NOTES

MISTAKE #2
NOT HAVING CLIENTS SIGN
A STATEMENT OF WORK

IN THE LAST CHAPTER, I shared with you that I made the mistake of not investing in a high-quality website when I started out on this journey to become a full-time copywriter and content writer. And while this mistake didn't necessarily keep me from finding success, it certainly created some headaches. This next mistake? I did not have clients sign a statement of work for my content writing services. Big mistake. Huge.

DO COPYWRITERS NEED A STATEMENT OF WORK?

Before I get into the details of what happened and what made me realize that I needed a master services agreement and statement of work, I want to level on a few things. First, as you probably know by now, I'm a huge advocate of Upwork—have I already said that? The Upwork platform helped me start as a revenue-making copywriter and content writer in 2019. So, when I started my S-Corp in March 2023, I initially assumed I would just keep getting clients through the same freelancing platform I always had.

To be clear, if you are a new copywriter, blog writer, or any kind of content writer and plan to use Upwork exclusively, this chapter doesn't necessarily apply to you. But I implore you to keep reading. If your business is anything like mine and starts to scale and grow, you may want to expand beyond the Upwork revenue stream.

If you do stick to Upwork exclusively, know that Upwork takes care of all of this for you. You have all the protections you need if you stick to the freelancer requirements. If clients engage freelancers, they agree to pay them for the work. If they fail to pay, Upwork will handle everything on your behalf. Plus, you get all the marketing, advertising, and payment processing benefits of using the tool.

If you plan to take on clients outside of Upwork, however, you need a statement of work and, more than likely, a master services agreement. What's the difference between the two? Here's the scoop:

WHAT IS A MASTER SERVICES AGREEMENT?

A Master Services Agreement (MSA) is a contract between you and your client that outlines the general terms and conditions of your working relationship. As a copywriter or content writer, this agreement covers important elements like payment terms, confidentiality, ownership of work, and how to handle any disputes that might arise.

The MSA sets the groundwork for your entire business relationship, making sure both parties understand their rights and responsibilities from the start. It's a great way to protect yourself and ensure everyone is on the same page before any specific projects begin.

WHAT IS A STATEMENT OF WORK?

A Statement of Work (SOW) outlines a project's specific tasks, deliverables, and deadlines. For copywriters and content writers, the SOW includes the type of content you'll create, the length, the format, and the timeline for delivery. It also specifies the cost and any milestones for payments. An SOW goes above and beyond a proposal document and provides you a bit more of a legal footing should things go wrong down the road.

The SOW works alongside the MSA, detailing the nitty-gritty of each project, while the MSA covers the overall relationship. Having clients sign an SOW ensures there's no confusion about what's expected, preventing misunderstandings and protecting you from scope creep.

To answer that question at the beginning of this chapter—do copywriters need a Statement of Work? YES!

THE BACKGROUND STORY: WHEN I REALIZED I NEEDED A LEGAL AGREEMENT IN PLACE

Shortly after turning my side hustle into a full-time gig, I had some prospective clients contact me via email or introductions from colleagues and acquaintances. In some cases, those clients were willing to head to Upwork, sign up for accounts, and engage with me that way. But others wanted a more direct relationship. At the time, I thought I had adequately weighed the pros and cons and decided that going direct was right.

Here are the benefits I considered when considering going directly with some clients vs. working with clients exclusively in Upwork.

- **More flexibility:** in communications: Upwork requires freelancers to communicate almost exclusively within the platform, which can be restrictive. Direct communication allows for quicker responses and more personalized interactions.

- **Make more money:** Upwork charges 10% of all freelancer revenues to help pay for the platform. By working directly with clients, I could avoid these fees and retain more of my earnings.

- **Build stronger client relationships:** Direct interactions often lead to stronger, more personal relationships with clients, building trust and potentially leading to long-term collaborations.

- **Greater control over projects:** Working outside of Upwork gives me more control over how I manage projects, set deadlines, and handle revisions, allowing me to tailor my approach to each client's needs.

But I was naive in all of this. I assumed that the old-school gentlemen's agreement of yesteryear would suffice. We agree to a rate, I provide the work, you agree to the deliverables and approve the deliverables, you pay me, and we move on. Unfortunately, it's not quite that simple. And I allowed myself to get burned—like I said before, to the tune of about three thousand dollars.

The moral of the story? A legal agreement does far more for you than agreeing on your rates and when you'll get paid in a more informal way. An SOW and the MSA that it hangs on also outline the specific deliverables, how the work gets done, and what approval of a work product looks like. It allows you to outline specific details and your approach to the job. It gets both parties on the same page so that there are no surprises.

THE KEY COMPONENTS OF A COPYWRITER MASTER SERVICES AGREEMENT

If you write for a client outside of a platform like Upwork or Fiverr, take the time to prepare a contract template. You can hire an attorney directly or sign up for a membership with a program such as LegalShield. Having a base contract drawn up is worth the financial investment, regardless of your approach. This becomes a template you can send prospective clients before agreeing to move forward with work.

If the contract is prepared well, you'll have to make very few edits to reach a final agreement. You can likely handle this without an attorney reviewing the proposed changes. Getting a base MSA and SOW template will likely cost you between $200 and $1,500. Mine came in just shy of $1,200 (though had I known about LegalShield sooner, I probably could have saved some money).

If you're doing the math, you've probably calculated that loss I mentioned earlier and realized that I wouldn't have lost that much money had I done the due diligence up front. Then again, my mistake gave me another topic to share with you.

Before we get into the key components of the SOW, let's talk about some of the unique things you will want to have in your MSA.

THE LEGALESE

Let's start with the legal components that your attorney will add. Your Master Services Agreement should outline basic obligations for both parties, ensuring clarity on what is expected. Indemnification clauses protect you from legal claims about the client's use of your work.

Limitation on liability keeps your potential damages within a reasonable range. The contract term specifies the length of the agreement, while termination clauses detail how either party can end the contract. Force majeure covers unforeseen events like natural disasters that might prevent you from fulfilling the contract. Finally, a clear process for dispute resolution should be included to handle any issues that arise professionally and efficiently.

RATES (HOW MUCH YOU GET PAID)

Contrary to what you might think, your rates are actually not listed in the Master Services Agreement (MSA). Instead, these are reserved for the schedule or Statement of Work (SOW). Why? Because your rates can change based on the type of project you do, and, if you are like most content writers, your rates will increase annually (the cost of living does, so your rates should, too).

With all this said, the MSA needs to include an agreement for payment and payment terms. It should outline the process for invoicing, payment deadlines, and penalties for late payments. I typically invoice twice a month or every 14 days, with payment due within 14 days of the invoice date. However, be prepared for some larger clients who have standard net 30 terms. It's essential to clearly state your terms in the MSA to avoid any confusion.

Your MSA should also address late payments. My agreement specifies that all current work will cease until outstanding invoices are paid. Additionally, I am entitled to an incremental fee for late invoices every two days. This clause helps clients take payment terms seriously and protects your business from cash flow issues. An estimated 82% of small businesses fail because of cash flow issues. Don't let yours be one of them.

COOPERATION AND COMMUNICATION

This is a big one. Make sure your MSA discusses what you expect from your client and not just what they should expect from you. One of the big things here is responsiveness and communication. Your client should be expected to respond to your questions and provide approval and feedback on your work in a reasonable period of time. My standard MSA requires two days. Let me tell you why.

About a year ago, I worked with an Upwork client on her resumé, cover letter, and some LinkedIn optimization. I spent several hours perfecting her resumé, drafting that initial cover letter, and updating her LinkedIn profile. At that point in time, I had a good handle on who she was as a professional. But, I had a few questions, and I needed her input to get the documents over the finish line. I sent her a list of questions through Upwork. And I heard nothing. Not for five months. Then, all of a sudden, I hear from her. She has some of the answers to my questions and new project requests.

You might think, okay, so make the changes. But the problem was, I barely remembered her at that point. It wasn't that I didn't care about the work, but I work on dozens of resumés, and I write well over 10,000 words a day on most days. I was no longer in the zone on her work, and getting back in the zone would take more time and effort than what she was paying me for.

Thankfully, I had clearly outlined in the Upwork contract that responses to questions were required within two days, and the entire project should take no more than five days. I politely explained this to her and shared that it would take me some time to review her initial input materials to gain context to those questions from so many months ago. Plus, she added scope that was not part of the initial request—this is called scope creep and it can be the kiss of death. But, because I had that all in writing, she was willing to pay for my additional time and effort.

This long-winded story explains why it is so important to outline your client's expectations. This can protect you in the long run. Here are some things to consider:

- **Response times:** Specify how quickly clients should respond to your questions or requests for information (e.g., within two days).

- **Approval process:** Clearly state how and when clients should provide feedback and approval on your work.

- **Project scope:** At a high level, indicate that additional scope will be billed for the incremental effort. You will specify more about the scope in your SOW.

- **Communication channels:** Agree on preferred communication methods (e.g., email, phone, or project management tools). I prefer email as it gives me a paper trail of my client communications.

- **Availability:** Outline the client's (and your) general availability for meetings or check-ins to ensure regular and productive communication.

- **Additional requests:** Specify how new project requests or additional work will be handled and billed.

- **Review periods:** Set timeframes for review and revisions to keep the project moving forward without unnecessary delays.

- **Escalation process:** Define a process for handling any issues or disputes that may arise during the project.

In the bullets above, I mentioned the importance of outlining the approval process. But this goes deeper than that. You must be clear on how you expect to receive approvals and what happens when you don't. For example, you might want to indicate that a client has five days to provide project approval after delivery. If you do not receive that requested approval, the project is considered approved, and you can move on.

Also, talk about what approval implies, and have this conversation verbally with your client as well. If they approve a project, they agree to the work as-is and have done all the due checks they require on their end. For my clients, this means that they agree the work is 100% original (I use Copyscape–a plagiarism checker––to confirm this with each deliverable) and aligns with any allowance of artificial intelligence that they have agreed to.

USE OF ARTIFICIAL INTELLIGENCE

Okay, I know the last part of that last sentence might have you thinking—what does artificial intelligence have to do with anything? Whether you use AI (ChatGPT, Jasper, etc.) or not, AI is a thing today, and many copywriters, myself included, use it. Though I try diligently to use it sparingly, I am finding that the work I have written with my own brain and my own hands is flagged as "likely to be generated by ChatGPT content."

This can be exceedingly frustrating. But even more frustrating can be a client returning to you weeks or months after approving the work and posting it to their website, now upset that it is flagging as AI, and wanting you to rewrite the work. Remember that three thousand dollar loss I talked about earlier in this article? Yep, that was related to AI. I'll share more about that in a subsequent chapter.

This chapter is intended to talk about the importance of an MSA and SOW, not about whether or not you use AI. However, I would do you a disservice if I didn't mention this here. Artificial intelligence is all around us. And in today's world, it can help content writers do their jobs faster and better.

Being upfront about your tool use is non-negotiable—and get it in writing. Don't rely on verbal conversations to agree about how AI will be used—or will not be used—because I highly believe that as more and more time goes on, it will be harder to get content to get through a tool as 100% human, even if it was indeed written 100% by a human.

My MSA says something similar to the following (feel free to borrow or steal):

Artificial Intelligence (AI) tools may occasionally be used to aid in creating content plans and outlines. In certain situations, AI may augment written content.

OWNERSHIP AND RIGHTS

Lastly, your MSA must outline who owns the work after you deliver it. This might vary depending on the type of writing you do, but in my case, I give my clients full rights to the work I do for them—after I receive their payment. This means that the work is my intellectual property even after they approve it, even if it is on their website until I receive payment. Once it is paid, it's theirs, and they can do with it however they wish.

Here are some ways clients might use the work I write for them once they have full rights:

- **Blogs:** Publishing articles and blog posts on their website.

- **Website Content:** Using the content on various pages of their website.

- **Company Presentations:** Including the content in internal or external company presentations.

- **Social Media:** Sharing the content on their social media platforms such as Facebook, their LinkedIn company page, X (formerly known as Twitter), Instagram, Pinterest, etc.

- **Flyers and Brochures:** Distributing the content through flyers, brochures, and other printed materials in the community.

- **Email Campaigns:** Using the content in email marketing campaigns to reach their audience.

- **Press Releases:** Including the content in press releases to announce company news or updates.

- **Advertising:** Using the content in online or print advertisements to promote their services or products.

THE KEY COMPONENTS OF A COPYWRITER STATEMENT OF WORK

With the right stuff in your MSA, your SOW is easy. And in case you have already forgotten, an SOW is a document that outlines a project's specific tasks, deliverables, and timelines. Here's what you need to include:

- **Rates:** Specify your rates for the project and note any anticipated rate increases as the partnership progresses. I increase my rates annually, usually in January.

- **Turn Times:** Outline the standard turnaround times for projects. For example, my standard turnaround time is seven days for small projects unless we agree otherwise.

- **Delivery Format:** Detail how the work will be delivered, such as a Google Doc, in SurferSEO or a similar tool, Microsoft Word, etc.

- **Scope of Work:** Clearly define the project's tasks and deliverables to avoid misunderstandings.

- **Milestones and Deadlines:** Set specific milestones and deadlines to keep the project on track.

- **Client Contact Information:** Include the client's contact details for easy communication.

- **Revisions:** State the number of revisions included and the request process.

- **Payment Terms:** Reiterate the payment terms and schedule from the MSA for clarity.

- **Project Timeline:** Provide an overall timeline for the project, including key dates and deadlines.

Today, all new clients that come to me outside of Upwork are asked to sign a contract. It's a requirement to move forward. Having an MSA and SOW in place is a must for protecting your business and establishing clear expectations with clients. These documents help prevent misunderstandings and ensure that both parties are on the same page regarding deliverables, payment terms, and communication protocols.

Don't make the same mistake I did. Invest the time and money to set up these agreements. This will allow you to avoid costly mistakes and focus on delivering high-quality work.

NOTES

MISTAKE #3
MISSTEPS IN PRICING—THE COST OF UNDERVALUING MY SERVICES

OKAY, AT THIS POINT I'VE TOLD YOU about how I went on the cheap and mistakenly invested in a poorly designed website (something I am happy to say is behind me now that my new website is up and running). I also shared with you my second mistake—failing to have clients sign an MSA and SOW, agreeing to the scope of our project. These were some pretty big doozies I paid dearly for last year.

And as you can guess from the title of this book, the mistakes didn't end there. So what was my third mistake? It was not charging what I am worth and the failure to create an established rate card for my business. And, as with many mistakes, this is still one I am working to correct today.

PRODUCT, PRICE, PROMOTION, AND PLACEMENT

If you've studied anything about marketing and advertising, you know it is all about product, price, promotion, and placement. In fact, I talked about these earlier in this book. Who knew we'd be back to talking about it now?

Of course, the pricing discussion really needs to start with the product. What is it that you are selling? In my case, I was and am selling my skills as a content writer. I am a copywriter and content writer who creates SEO-optimized content to help businesses drive more website traffic.

That type of service—a.k.a. my product—doesn't come for free. In fact, it can come at quite a premium, especially if you want high-quality content that doesn't sound like a robot wrote it and isn't full of grammatical and typographical errors.

So, how do you determine the right price for your product, especially when it's a service? When I started as a copywriter back in 2019, I charged just 4 cents per word. At that time, this was the cost of entry. While I had all the right skills, I needed to develop a reputation in the marketplace to command a higher rate down the road.

By early 2023, I was charging nine cents a word, and very shortly after, I brought it up to 10 cents per word. Today, I charge more than that for content writing and have aligned with copywriter best practices to establish a fixed fee for copywriting. Why the increase? Raising rates can help weed out low-quality work and attract more meaningful and rewarding projects. As you build your portfolio and client base, you can justify higher rates by showcasing the value and quality of your work. Pricing is not just about covering costs; it's about positioning yourself as a professional who delivers highly valued services worth paying for.

While I will tell you more about my specific mistakes related to pricing later in this article, I want to take some time to dive deeper into how copywriters should approach pricing their services, especially when first getting started. Honestly, I wish I had someone who taught me all this back in 2019. Who knows how much more revenue I could have brought in or how many more high-quality clients I could have secured?

PRICING YOURSELF AS A COPYWRITER

Labeling your service can make this whole pricing situation that much more complicated. And in many ways, it boils down to semantics. Are you a copywriter? Or are you a content writer? While these two "jobs" are similar, they're a bit different when you get down to it.

COPYWRITER VS. CONTENT WRITER

As Neil Patel puts it, copywriters create copy that sells—the text on your website that drives conversions, turning browsers into buyers. These are the words that tell the story in digital ads, on billboards, on emails, and so much more. Copywriters craft persuasive messages designed to drive actions, such as purchasing or signing up for a newsletter.

Content writers, on the other hand, create helpful content that helps a client to solve a problem. It engages and informs your audience. This includes blog posts, articles, eBooks, and social media updates. Content writers work to help build relationships with the audience, providing helpful information that keeps readers coming back for more. It's about building trust in customers through your content's expertise, experience, and authority—yes, that's my little plug for Google's EEAT (Experience, Expertise, Authority, and Trust) methodology. But that's a topic for another chapter, or even another book.

PAYCHECKS AND PERCEPTION

What's the difference between copywriting and content writing when it comes to paychecks? While you can make a great living content writing, copywriters generally get paid more.

This is because they play a direct role in facilitating sales and revenue in an organization. Their words drive conversions, making their work highly valuable to businesses looking to grow their bottom line. And trust me, if you are a great copywriter, you can totally command a premium rate. Why? Because the words you write for your client can help generate thousands and thousands of dollars. You shouldn't do that work for free.

WHY I CALL MYSELF A COPYWRITER

This all said, most of my work is content writing—it's what I love to do—yet I call myself a copywriter. Why? I'll be honest, many clients don't know the difference between the two roles. By identifying as a copywriter, I can leverage both skill sets, offering a full range of services and not getting pigeonholed into just the content space.

Today, I charge more than that for content writing and have aligned with copywriter best practices to establish a fixed fee for copywriting.

Positioning myself as a copywriter allows me to charge higher rates and demonstrate my role in driving client results. It positions me as versatile, flexible, and far more valuable than just one or the other.

WHAT'S THE RIGHT PRICE?

And now, back to our topic at hand of pricing yourself as a copywriter. The truth is that there are a lot of approaches to take, and my approach might not be the best one for you. But I am going to tell you the path I took to get where I am today, with a healthy salary that continues to grow.

I won't tell you what I brought in during 2023 or even what happened in 2024. Yet, since many copywriters will share articles on helpful tips on how to earn a six-figure salary as a copywriter, I'll tell you that I am there and more.

STARTING LOW AND CLIMBING THE LADDER

So how did I get here? As I shared earlier, when I started copywriting as a side hustle in 2019, I was charging just four cents a word. I knew at the time that I was on the low end, but the fact was that I needed to get some clients. I gradually increased my rates from four cents to seven cents, then to nine cents, and eventually ten cents per word. Today, I charge twelve cents per word, which is a good place to be—for now.

Author's Note: This rate is based on 2024 rates and I typically raise my rates in January of each year.

MARKET RESEARCH AND RATE SETTING

To establish my rates, I conducted extensive market research. According to research from Peak Freelance, 91% of writers in their first year make less than $30k, and 50% of writers have worked six to ten years to get into the $100k club. Thankfully, that's not me, so I must be doing something right—for now. It's just that I waited too long to get to where I am, and maybe I'm waiting too long for that next rate increase.

COMMON RATES AMONG FREELANCERS

Here are some common rates that you might see among other freelancers as of late 2024/early 2025:

- **Entry Level:** $.03 to $.06 per word

- **Intermediate:** $.07 to $.12 per word

- **Experienced:** $.13 to $.20 per word

- **Expert Level:** $.21 to $.30 per word

While I consider myself at the experienced to expert level, I know I'm sitting at the high end of that intermediate level. Why? Because it's all about supply and demand. I have a regular stream of work coming in and don't need to spend much time marketing my services. But perhaps most interesting is that when I was priced below 10 cents per word, I had to sell myself, hard. Interesting, isn't it?

HOW TO KNOW WHEN TO RE-EVALUATE YOUR PRICING STRATEGY

I know I framed up this chapter about my mistakes with pricing. And it's true. I waited too long to increase my prices when business picked up. Who knows how much money I left on the table! Well, I know—it was thousands of dollars.

But deciding how and when to change your pricing strategy can be complicated. You worry that you're changing your prices too often or not enough. You might worry about how your clients will respond.

However, it's important to understand that your clients are increasing their prices, too. Actually, everyone is increasing their prices. Groceries are more expensive. Putting gas in your car costs more than ever (or at least it seems that way). Utility prices are on the rise. The message? It's expensive to live.

And what do sellers do when creating their product or service starts to cost them more? They increase their prices. So it stands to reason that we, as copywriters, can do the same.

But a disorganized approach can get you into trouble. It can make your rates unpredictable and cause discord with your clients. Here's what I've learned about how and when to increase those prices:

- **Evaluate Annually:** Review your rates and expenses at least once a year. I now increase my rates annually—in January of each year.

- **Set Clear Guidelines:** I specify that the maximum yearly rate increase is 5% in my contract. Does this mean I will always increase my rate by 5%? Of course not, but it offers me some protection and flexibility.

- **Communicate Early:** Inform your clients about potential rate increases well in advance. This transparency helps maintain trust and allows them to budget accordingly.

- **Reflect in Your SOW and Service Agreements:** Your prices (and approach to rate increases) should be clearly outlined in your Statement of Work (SOW) and service agreements. This ensures that both you and your clients are on the same page and reduces the likelihood of disputes.

THE GRANDFATHERING APPROACH TO YOUR PRICING STRATEGY

Have you ever heard someone say, "Oh, we'll grandfather you in at the original rate?" This is a relatively common practice for sellers of all types of products and services. But it can get you into some trouble if you don't have a set strategy for how and when you'll start bringing those prices closer to your current published rates. We'll talk about the concept of a rate card shortly.

You might consider grandfathering in a client at old rates for many reasons. Here's how I have approached it.

Respect for Loyal Clients: Honoring lower rates for clients who helped me get my start shows appreciation for their loyalty and support during my early days.

- **Exploring New Niches:** Offering discounted rates allowed me to explore new niches and industries I might not have experience in, which helps expand my portfolio. Note: Notice the past tense of allowed, not allows, in that earlier sentence.

- **Securing Long-term Projects:** Sometimes, offering a lower rate can secure a long-term project or retainer, providing steady income and building a stronger client relationship. I'll talk about this more in a bit.

- **Building Trust:** Maintaining lower rates for certain clients can build trust and goodwill, create a positive working relationship, and encourage referrals.

- **Testing New Services:** Providing lower rates can be useful when testing new services or offerings, allowing for valuable feedback and adjustments without the pressure of higher prices.

While I don't have any clients at my original rates, I have some at slightly discounted rates for these reasons. This approach has allowed me to grow my business while respecting and valuing my relationships with long-standing clients. However, I know I can't keep those clients at those rates forever. More importantly, they know it, too—and they don't expect me to.

GETTING "OLDER" CLIENTS TO PAY YOUR "NEWER RATES"

When you're a small business owner like myself, you might feel bad when you need to communicate a price increase. However, no client will expect you to stay at those low rates forever. They're not doing that in their business, so they shouldn't (and likely don't) expect you to do that either. I suggest you work to get your long-term (those who have been around awhile) clients to your current rates sooner rather than later.

Here's why.

- **Fair Compensation for Your Work:** Continuing to charge old rates undervalues your skills and the quality of work you provide. Ensuring clients pay your current rates means you are fairly compensated for your time and expertise.

- **Avoiding Burnout:** Locking yourself into a long-term project at a low rate means you're doing the same amount of work that you could be doing for a new client at your new rate. This costs you money and can lead to burnout and dissatisfaction with your work.

- **Maintaining Business Growth:** Consistently working at old rates can hinder your business growth. As your expenses and experience grow, your rates should reflect that to maintain profitability and allow for future investments in your business.

- **Setting a Professional Precedent:** Keeping clients at outdated rates sets a precedent that your rates are negotiable or static. This can lead to the undervaluation of your services and make future rate increases even more challenging.

- **Encouraging Client Respect:** Clients who value and respect your work will understand the need for rate increases. Communicating these changes professionally reinforces your value and ensures that clients who stay with you are those who appreciate your expertise.

CREATING A RATE CARD AS PART OF YOUR COPYWRITING PRICING STRATEGY

I pride myself on being a smart person, yet I didn't think about creating a rate card until earlier this year. To borrow words from Pretty Woman, that was a "Big mistake. Huge."

There are prices everywhere—at the grocery store, at the local department store, even at your favorite spa. They're either listed on a board on the wall, a flyer, or the product itself. So why shouldn't you have some way to share your prices, too? This helps avoid questions and gets everyone on the same page. For copywriters, this means creating a rate card.

WHAT IS A RATE CARD?

A rate card is a menu of your services and their associated costs. It provides potential clients with a clear understanding of what you offer and how much it will cost them. This transparency helps manage client expectations and positions you as a professional who values your time and expertise and wants clients to do the same.

HOW TO PREPARE A RATE CARD

- **List Your Services:** Start by listing all the services you offer. This could include blog posts, website copy, social media content, email marketing, etc.

- **Set Clear Prices:** For each service, specify the price per word, per hour, or per project. Be clear and concise to avoid confusion.

- **Include Package Deals:** Consider offering package deals for clients who need multiple services. This can make your offerings more attractive and provide added value.

- **Highlight Your Expertise:** Use your rate card to showcase your expertise and experience. Include brief descriptions of each service and any relevant credentials or accomplishments.

- **Update Regularly:** Review and update your rate card regularly to reflect any changes in your pricing strategy or services offered.

SHARING YOUR RATE CARD

Your rate card should be shared with every new or prospective client. This creates transparency from the get-go and sets the stage for your annual rate increases. By providing a rate card, you eliminate guesswork and ensure that your clients are fully aware of your pricing structure from the start. It also makes communicating any future rate changes easier, as clients will already be familiar with your professional approach to pricing.

A CLEAR COPYWRITING PRICING STRATEGY SETS YOU UP FOR SUCCESS

The pricing mistake has been a big one and one I am still figuring out today. However, one thing I have learned is that my clients appreciate my transparency. In fact, I've had some rather enlightening conversations with clients who were just waiting for those increases to come, and they didn't bat an eyelash.

The message? Think through your approach to pricing from the start. Document it, communicate it, and refine it as your business grows. And be sure to charge for the value that you provide. It'll be worth it and in more than just your paycheck.

NOTES

MISTAKE #4
NOT SPENDING ENOUGH TIME ON LEAD GENERATION FOR COPYWRITERS

"IF YOU BUILD IT, THEY WILL COME." Okay, I had to start this chapter with this infamous quote from the Kevin Costner film, "Field of Dreams". That line, ominously stated by Ray Liotta in the 1989 films, often resonates in my head. And ironically, as I am editing this chapter today, the news came that actor James Earl Jones has passed away. One of his famous lines in that film was, "people will come."

Now, I'll admit, I'm a huge Kevin Costner fan. "The Guardian" is one of my all-time favorite movies—yes, I know it ends badly. I also love "Hidden Figures", "Message in a Bottle", "The Bodyguard"… My list of favorite Costner flicks could go on and on. But that's not the topic of this chapter. Lead generation, however, is.

What do those quotes from Ray Liotta and James Earl Jones have to do with lead generation? In the film, it means that if you put in the effort to build something worthwhile, people will naturally come to it. It's a nice sentiment, but in the world of copywriting, it's not enough to just set up your website and hope clients will find you. That's why lead generation—a.k.a. lead development—is integral to growing your business.

MY EARLY INTRODUCTION TO LEAD GENERATION FOR COPYWRITERS

Let's go back in time a bit to when I started my side hustle back in 2019. As I have shared in previous chapters and some interviews I have done with members of the press, I have always loved to write. And in 2019, I went through a career change and the golden opportunity to start freelancing finally became something I just couldn't pass up.

Naturally, I decided to create a freelancer profile on Upwork. I set it up. I waited. And nothing happened.

While I assumed that since I had all this great experience and had set up a pretty strong profile—or so I thought—the leads would just start rolling in. But they didn't. Why? Because I was doing nothing. I had let myself forget what the platform was all about. Though, yes, it is a marketing and advertising tool, there were thousands and thousands of freelancers out there all vying for attention. This means that free-lancers—myself included—needed to take steps to rise to the top of the list.

I needed to go out and bid for work, and I needed to do it often. While we can talk at another time about how you might need to "un-dersell" yourself initially to start collecting some feedback, the point is that you need to sell yourself. Once I started doing that, those leads started rolling in. Some of those clients I still write for today.

WHY I FORGOT THAT LEAD DEVELOPMENT WAS SO IMPORTANT

Let's fast forward again. Now we're sitting in January of 2023 as I contemplate turning my side hustle into a full-time gig. While I still had an active Upwork profile, I hadn't really spent any time improving it in recent years. Full-time employment and some big life changes had gotten in the way—don't worry, those of you who read *Perseverance. Reinvention.*, know that it all ended well.

That said, I had still been using the Upwork platform to communicate with clients, but it was really just being used as a communication tool and payment processing platform.

Now I was in a situation where I needed to grow that client base quickly. To make that happen, I did a couple of things. First, I started contacting my existing client base to see if they had more work for me. Surprisingly, they all did, and my pipeline grew quickly. However, I still had an income gap of about 40% compared to where I had been when employed full-time with copywriting as a side gig. And with a severance package ending in just a couple of months, I needed to work quickly to fill that gap and avoid unemployment.

Aside from reaching out to existing clients, I also took a seminar from another copywriter who had gone down a similar path just a few years before. Her business had grown exponentially, and she was quite the role model for me. Her seminar series helped me dust off my Upwork profile to make some improvements (helpful hint: Upwork seems to add new fields to the profile section occasionally, so be sure your profile is always up to date).

While I was taking the seminar, I submitted proposal after proposal and eventually, that income gap got smaller and smaller. By the end of March 2023, I had so much work coming in that I stopped doing something super important—I stopped sending proposals.

LEAD DEVELOPMENT & LEAD GENERATION NEVER ENDS

I'm not kidding. I was blissfully overwhelmed by so much work, and I wasn't getting small leads. There were some whales coming in, some of which paid more than the rate I was currently charging.

But here's the thing: things change. They really do. And those changes can often come without notice. Projects can end abruptly in the world of freelance work, especially on platforms like Upwork or Fiverr. Clients can decide to pause work, shift priorities, or even run out of budget. This can leave you hanging, especially if you're working at an hourly rate. One day, you might have a full schedule; the next, your calendar could be wide open.

This has happened to me a couple of times. I had clients who suddenly decided to cut back on their projects or stop altogether. Remember how I mentioned I had some whales (for those of you without a sales background, a whale is a client with the potential of bringing you some seriously big revenue)? Well, the biggest white whale of them all suddenly had to scale back—big time.

Sometimes, pulling back is out of your client's control, and sometimes, it's just the nature of the business. That's why it's so important to keep your pipeline full and always look for new opportunities. Never assume that your current workload will stay the same forever. Because guess what happened when that whale disappeared? I didn't have prospects waiting in the pipeline.

HOW TO DRIVE LEAD GENERATION FOR COPYWRITERS

Let's talk a bit about how to drive lead generation, especially business-to-business (B2B) lead generation, for copywriters. As you know by now, I realized that Upwork alone wouldn't cut it. I needed to branch out.

If you are a new copywriter or content writer looking to grow your business, I suggest you branch out, too. Just be sure you do a few things before you get too far. The first is to invest in a good starter website. The next is to have an attorney or organization help you create a contract and statement of work to use with those non-Upwork clients. Finally, do a pricing assessment to make sure you are pricing your copywriting and content-writing services accordingly.

STEPS TO GENERATE NEW CONTENT LEADS

Whether you are a copywriter or content writer, you know that your business doesn't result in sales similar to the commission a real estate agent or car salesperson might achieve. While copywriting can generate thousands of dollars for great content that drives conversions, content writing isn't always as profitable—unless you know how to do it right by following those tips I mentioned earlier and staying on top of your lead generation efforts.

And so, without further ado, here's what you need to do to keep that pipeline healthy:

- **Network Consistently:** Join online communities, attend industry events, and connect with fellow freelancers. Networking can lead to referrals and collaborations.

- **Optimize Your Website:** Make sure your website is user-friendly and optimized for search engines. Include a blog to showcase your expertise and use SEO techniques to attract organic traffic.

- **Maximize Social Media:** Use platforms like LinkedIn, Twitter, Instagram, and even Pinterest to share your work, connect with potential clients, and engage with your audience. Regularly posting and interacting will keep you on the radar. I'll discuss this in a subsequent chapter.

- **Cold Outreach:** Don't hesitate to reach out directly to potential clients. Research companies that might need your services and send personalized emails explaining how you can help them. LinkedIn is a great way to do this.

- **Maintain an Updated Portfolio:** Regularly update your portfolio with recent work. Upwork provides an easy way for you to update your profile. I also keep an old-fashioned Word document with links to some of my past client work. I send it along with every proposal. My prospective clients love it.

- **Ask for Referrals:** Don't hesitate to ask your current clients for referrals. They'll likely recommend you to others if they're happy with your work. I have received a lot of new work through referrals.

- **Use Those Freelance Platforms Wisely:** Platforms like Upwork and Fiverr can be great for finding new clients. Make sure your profile is up to date, and submit proposals regularly.

- **Follow Up on Old Leads:** Revisit old leads or past clients who may have only temporarily needed your services. A friendly check-in can often lead to new opportunities.

TIME MANAGEMENT AND PRODUCTIVITY TIPS FOR EFFECTIVE LEAD GENERATION

Okay, so I know what you're thinking—all these lead-generation efforts are going to be time-consuming. And you're right. They are. The fact is that B2B lead generation takes work. Yet, I'll tell you that if you organize your day right, it doesn't need to be a time suck. In fact, it might become a part of your day that you will enjoy immensely.

How do I manage lead generation today? I'm so glad you asked!

If you have read any of the posts on my blog, you know that I have established some boundaries on my workday. These aren't barriers, but boundaries that allow me to be as productive as possible. I know I'm not a morning person, and I'm just not creative before about 11 a.m. That's just me and who I am. So I have established writing hours that don't start until a time that is conducive to my creative brain because when you're in the content writing business, you're in trouble if the words won't come.

I also limit my client calls to just two days a week. Clients can schedule calls with me on Tuesdays and Thursdays between 11 a.m. and 4 p.m. I do this so that I can stay focused on creating my best work on my other work days. Of course, the beauty of self-employment, especially as a writer, is that I can change my writing hours at any time, depending on my mood and my other life responsibilities.

FOCUS ON LEAD MANAGEMENT AT THE BEGINNING AND END OF THE WRITING DAY

I know you want me to get to the question—how do I manage lead generation today? It's simple. I use the time in the mornings before I begin writing to go through my emails and respond to anything waiting for a response, check for proposal opportunities in Upwork, and look for new gigs that might be posted on the Upwork platform.

I do the same thing at the end of the day (which, yes, might be at 11 p.m. based on my day). This ensures that I promptly respond to prospective clients without leaving them waiting. Responsiveness is one of my value propositions, and I take it very seriously.

But the key here is to figure out what works for you. If you keep starting and stopping your writing projects to check for leads and write proposals, you may end up delivering less work than what you are capable of. So take time to look at how you approach your day and set aside time to focus on new leads. And remember, no matter how full your pipeline is, treat every opportunity as revenue potential. Trust me, you'll figure it out, and it's a good problem to have.

BUILDING LONG-TERM CLIENT RELATIONSHIPS

Part of the mistake I made when I failed to understand the importance of daily lead generation was forgetting the value of my existing client relationships. Let me first clarify what I mean by that. Obviously, my long-term client relationships are super important to me. They've been a consistent source of revenue and feedback that has helped me grow my business and let me do what I love to do every day.

However, I forgot something that I learned in all those sales trainings so many years ago and throughout my career—yes, I have been in the sales space, so my experience with sales methodologies such as BANT (budget, authority, needs, and timeline) and the Miller-Heiman approach has definitely paid off for me here. I forgot that my existing client base can also be a source of incremental revenue.

FIVE THINGS TO HELP GROW THOSE EXISTING CLIENT RELATIONSHIPS AND BRING IN MORE REVENUE

Here are some simple things you can do to help grow revenue with those clients who have helped you get where you are. And the great thing is that most of these tips don't take long—plus, they'll help you grow your skills and become more valuable to your clients.

- **Conduct Website Reviews:** Offer to review their website periodically—or just do it yourself. Focus on areas you can improve, such as copy updates, SEO enhancements, or content refreshes. If there are areas outside your expertise, like design or technical SEO, I suggest partnering with other marketing professionals to fill those gaps.

- **Suggest New Projects:** Proactively suggest new work based on their current needs or industry trends. This could include creating new blog posts or increasing the cadence and frequency, updating case studies, updating old posts that are now out of date, launching email campaigns, or developing new marketing materials.

- **Follow Up Regularly:** When clients go quiet, don't assume they no longer need your services. They might just be busy or thought they had sent you a project, but it is sitting in their draft bin—I literally have a client like this today who just gets so bogged down in the day-to-day that he forgets to send me the work for the week. Reach out with a friendly check-in to see how they're doing and if there's anything you can assist with. This keeps you top-of-mind and can often lead to new projects.

- **Offer Additional Services:** Expand your services to include things like social media post development and management, content strategy, or even coaching sessions. I recently started offering this to some of my clients, offering to upload approved content to their Wordpress site to help them grow visibility. In fact, this is a great strategy that can help you grow your revenue fast. Write the blogs, post the content to the client's website, and then write social media posts that feature the blog and draw customers back to your client's website. It's a win-win-win value proposition.

- **Request Referrals:** I mentioned this one earlier, but here is where it can really pay off. While you can attend networking events, meet new people, and ask for referrals, you're far more likely to get those referrals from your long-standing clients. Encourage satisfied clients to refer you to others. You can even offer short-term incentives like discounts on future projects or a referral bonus to motivate them—the keyword here is short-term. Refrain from over-discounting your services or grandfathering in clients at a lower rate for too long.

DEALING WITH REJECTION AND STAYING MOTIVATED

At this point, I think you get it. Lead generation needs to be part of your copywriting and content-writing process. But I want to be very clear here: You won't win every deal that you submit a proposal to. In fact, you'll lose far more than you'll win. And you might not even hear responses when you submit a proposal. It's a sad part of the business and just something you must be prepared for.

There are many reasons why you might not win a proposal. Sometimes, it's about pricing. Your rates might be too high or too low compared to the competition. Timing can also be a factor; maybe the client needed someone to start immediately, and you weren't available. A poorly written proposal can also hurt your chances. Make sure your proposals are clear, concise, and tailored to each client's needs. Using tools like Loom to create personalized video proposals can set you apart and add a personal touch.

The overall competition is another significant factor. According to Zippia, there are 4,882 freelance copywriters currently employed in the United States as of the time I wrote this chapter—but I suspect that number is actually quite higher. And worldwide, hundreds of thousands or even millions of freelancers are competing for similar projects.

Even if you never receive feedback on why you didn't win a proposal, take each experience as a learning opportunity. Reflect on what you could improve next time. Was your pricing competitive? Did you showcase relevant experience? Was your proposal well-written and engaging? Constantly refine your approach based on these reflections.

Remember, rejection is part of the process. Stay motivated by setting small, achievable goals and celebrating your successes, no matter how small. Keep honing your skills, learning from each experience, and maintaining a positive outlook. It's worth it.

LEAD DEVELOPMENT IS AN ITERATIVE AND ONGOING PROCESS

Lead generation is a continuous process that demands perseverance—you'll learn that perseverance is one of my favorite words—and strategic effort. Don't let setbacks discourage you; every experience is a stepping stone to success.

NOTES

MISTAKE #5

NOT LOOKING OUT FOR MY BUSINESS WITH BUSINESS LIABILITY INSURANCE

I ALREADY KNOW WHAT YOU'RE THINKING because I had this same question when the concept first surfaced for me: Just what is business liability insurance? And why does a copywriter or freelance blogger need it, especially if they are working on a platform such as Upwork or have put an MSA and SOW in place with their client? Well, I'm going to tell you all about it.

Business liability insurance is a type of coverage that protects your business from claims that can arise from your day-to-day operations. These claims could be for mistakes in your work, injuries, or property damage. Even as a copywriter or freelance blogger, these risks can pop up when you least expect them.

For instance, imagine you write a blog post for a client, but a mistake that no one caught leads to a legal issue for them. They might sue you for damages, which can be a risk, especially if you don't have a services agreement in place.

Or a client visits your home office for a meeting and slips on your icy driveway, injuring themselves. Or your laptop gets stolen from your bag when you are at a networking event—this would be a nightmare for any content writer who takes her laptop anywhere she goes. And good laptops don't come cheap.

These scenarios might seem far-fetched, but they can and do happen. Without business liability insurance, you could be personally responsible for covering the costs of these claims. This could mean paying for legal fees, medical bills, or even out-of-pocket settlement costs.

DO COPYWRITERS REALLY NEED BUSINESS LIABILITY INSURANCE?

So, why do copywriters and freelance bloggers need this insurance? Simply put, it's a safety net. It protects your finances and your reputation. When you're just starting, it's easy to think you won't need it because you're working on a small scale or from the comfort of your home.

But the truth is one big claim can put you out of business. Having business liability insurance shows that you are professional and prepared for anything. And I know this begs the question—what made me realize I might benefit from this insurance and sleep better at night? Read on. I'll tell you.

MY STORY: WHY I'LL NEVER OPERATE WITHOUT BUSINESS LIABILITY INSURANCE AGAIN

Okay, let's be clear from the get-go: I have never been sued. So, if you were starting to worry about me being involved in some legal action, you can let that go. However, I did have a client threaten legal action. And while they didn't have a case—I did consult with a few connections in the legal business to confirm that—it raised my hackles a bit.

I was introduced to this client through another connection. I'll be honest, it was super exciting. It was the largest referral I had received to date. And this client wanted a lot of content, and he wanted it fast. I won't name the client, but I will share that his business sells corrugated metal roofing, siding, and fencing products across North America. It's a pretty cool business, as he has invested a lot of money into creating an excellent product that is built to last.

Before I was introduced to the client, I had a quick call with his SEO consultant. That call was requested urgently, and my only option to take the call that day was from my car on my way to an event. (Note to readers: Never rush an onboarding or prospect call). I could not take notes, the connection wasn't the best, and we had no written follow-up from the call. Mistake after mistake after mistake. And during the call, I mentioned that I would leverage artificial intelligence from time to time and where needed to help augment the content. That was that.

BUILDING MY CONTENT ON THE WRONG BASELINE

Here's what happened next. First, I didn't have a contract in place with the client—a big mistake. Second, I let myself build the framework for future content for this client based on content already on his site—and all of that content was AI-generated.

Here's the thing. I wrote most of the content for this client on my own. Me and my brain leveraged insights that the client had provided me that were specific to his business. This content could not be written by an AI tool because it was unique to his business. But I'll be clear—construction and corrugated metal products are not really my specialty. So I leveraged AI to help me write use cases and explain how these products could be used across various projects.

The client loved my work. I received note after note thanking me for the great work and requesting more and more. And, long story short,

Google came out with an algorithm announcement in March 2024. The client panicked.

Even though his content started appearing on the first page of search results and was specific and unique to his business—and 100% original, I might add—he worried that his investment in content would go down the toilet. And while that was not and would not be the case for him—which was explained to him by his SEO consultant—he just wasn't having it. So, he threatened legal action if I didn't rewrite the content.

GET EXPECTATIONS IN WRITING

The moral of this particular story is to get expectations in writing. I failed to follow up with the SEO consultant to recap our conversation. I also failed to clarify with the client that he was okay with using AI to help generate and augment content for his website. Even though his site was full of AI-generated content, I failed to confirm that it was acceptable moving forward. This was a big learning opportunity for me. Refer back to chapter two for those insights I shared about legal contracts.

Though this chapter is intended to talk about business liability insurance, and I promise we'll get back to that shortly, I know you want to know what happened next.

Here's what I did—I rewrote all the content. All of it. It was relatively easy since I had written it in the first place but had used AI to rewrite much of it to make it more technical and "construction-friendly." Rewriting it was the right thing to do.

Here is where I screwed up. When the client threatened legal action, I freaked out. I let it get in my head and failed to read his request. I scanned his note, my hands shaking, and interpreted his request that he was going to sue me, and expected me to rewrite the content, and expected a monetary credit for the work done so far. I misread, thinking he wanted all of those things.

So what did I do? I responded quickly with a rebuttal. I apologized for the misunderstanding, reiterated the conversation with the consultant, and offered to rewrite the content and offer a credit—to the tune of about $3,000. I went overboard. I would have realized I didn't need to do all that if I had just slowed down a bit.

BUSINESS LIABILITY INSURANCE AND PEACE OF MIND

We'll get to the components of business liability insurance shortly, but first, let's talk about a few other important things. When working with clients, you must put ethics and responsibility first in everything you do. Be upfront about your approach to writing, and make sure you get an agreement in writing. Always have a statement of work in place. Here's the thing: Some clients love AI, while others want nothing to do with it. As a copywriter and content writer, you must respect that and get everything on the table.

Had I gotten this in writing or sent that meeting recap after that evening call with the consultant, I would have learned that while their site was full of AI content, they wanted something other than AI content from me—and I would have known to use an AI checker to check double (yes, sometimes these AI checkers get it wrong). It would have been an easy solution. But I didn't do that. And though I find it oddly humorous that the writing on their site since I have stopped writing for them is once again flagging as AI, that's beside the point.

The key here is to start with ethics. Be upfront about what you do. Charge appropriate rates. Make sure you understand the client's expectations and go from there. When you do that, situations like this won't happen.

So, if you practice ethics in everything you do, why do you still need this insurance? The answer is simple: Things can still go wrong even when you do everything right. A client might misunderstand a part of your agreement, or an unexpected accident could occur. Business liability insurance is there to protect you when the unexpected happens. It gives you peace of mind, knowing that you're covered in case something goes wrong, allowing you to focus on what you do best—writing great content for your clients.

WHAT DOES BUSINESS LIABILITY INSURANCE FOR FREELANCE BLOGGERS INCLUDE?

Okay, let's get to it and help you further understand why I have business liability insurance. Here's what this type of policy typically covers:

- **Legal Action:** If a client sues you and proves damages, the insurance can help pay for legal fees and any settlements or judgments against you.

- **Property Damage:** If your laptop gets stolen or damaged, the insurance can help cover the cost of repair or replacement.

- **Work-Related Accidents:** If you're in an accident while traveling for work, the insurance can help pay for car repairs.

- **Advertising Injuries:** This includes things like libel (writing something false about someone), slander (saying something false about someone), and trademark or copyright infringement (using someone else's trademark or copyrighted material without permission).

- **Professional Errors (Errors and Omissions Insurance):** This covers freelancers accused of making a professional error, such as delivering work that's late or incomplete, making a mistake in your work, or being negligent in performing your work.

- **Data Breach Protection:** One of the biggest risks for freelancers working online is a data breach, which can be very expensive. Now, in my case, I don't keep or collect sensitive customer data such as credit card numbers. But that's not to say that you won't. Cybersecurity insurance can help pay for notifying affected customers, forensic services to determine how the breach occurred, legal services to comply with regulations, customer credit and fraud monitoring services, and business interruption expenses.

- **Business Interruption Insurance:** If an unexpected event, like a riot or theft, prevents you from doing business, this insurance can help cover lost income, taxes, relocation costs, and lease payments. However, we should know that not all natural disasters are covered under this type of policy. So, if your freelance business is in an area prone to flooding, you might need a separate policy.

HOW MUCH DOES BUSINESS LIABILITY INSURANCE FOR COPYWRITERS COST?

If you're like me when I first started realizing I might want the peace of mind that business liability insurance can provide, you might want to know how much it costs. And I know you're going to hate this answer—it depends. There are a lot of things that go into determining how much you're going to pay.

The underwriter is going to consider the type of business you are in, the years you've been doing it, past claims, the amount of risk you are susceptible to, how much coverage you want, and even where your business is based. But here's the good news: Business liability insurance for freelance bloggers and copywriters doesn't cost as much as you might think.

BUSINESS LIABILITY INSURANCE IS A WORTHWHILE INVESTMENT

The Hartford underwrote my policy, and I am paying under the estimated average of $805 annually. And that's the cost of just a small handful of blogs. So, it's an easy expense to bite off—at least in my opinion. Plus, the truth is that as copywriters, especially when we have a service agreement in place, we just don't open ourselves up to that much liability.

Here's why:

- Most of us work from home.

- Copywriting is generally considered a low-risk industry compared to fields like construction or healthcare.

- We have contracts that protect us.

- Clients are responsible for verifying the factuality and applicability of the content.

- Our work typically doesn't involve physical products or face-to-face customer interactions.

- We usually don't have a lot of expensive equipment or inventory that needs to be covered. For me, it's just my laptop and a monitor. And, yes, while I have vlogging equipment, it doesn't go anywhere.

- Most of our work is digital, reducing the risk of physical loss or damage.

- Many copywriters work solo or with a small team, so potential employee-related claims are limited.

- We rarely have clients visit our home offices, so there is a low risk of on-site accidents. For my business, if I am going to meet a client, it is always in a public place and never in my home.

THE MORAL OF THE STORY: BUSINESS LIABILITY INSURANCE FOR CONTENT WRITERS

If you made it this far in the chapter. I think I know what you are thinking.

You're questioning your processes and making sure you are covering all the bases during your blog scoping calls. You're wondering if you are capturing requirements accurately and getting expectations in writing. Maybe you are thinking it is time to leverage an attorney to get a general contract that you can use for future client onboarding.

It's natural for all these things to be going through your head. These are common thoughts that all copywriters have when starting their businesses. Lastly, you are wondering if you can afford all of these expenses that it takes to set up a business the right way.

I mean, think about it.

- Your website could cost you $3,000 or more to get it done right the first time.

- There are costs associated with getting great imagery for your website and promotional materials. One professional photo and video shoot can easily cost $3,000 or more.

- Depending on the scope of your work, getting a contract template from a legal firm can cost anywhere from $2000 to several thousand dollars.

- Business liability insurance is about $800 a year.

And what about all those other expenses that you take on as a copywriter?

- Subscriptions to publications that you might need access to for research.
- Software and tools for writing, editing, and project management.
- Marketing and advertising costs to promote your services.
- Professional development courses and certifications.
- Office supplies and equipment upgrades.
- Travel expenses for client meetings or conferences.
- Website maintenance and hosting fees.
- Membership fees for professional organizations.

The costs add up. But, investing in insurance, in my opinion, is just one of those things you need to do to protect your business for the long haul. Try to move insurance higher up your priority list and make it an annual cost that simply becomes part of your budget without the need to think twice. Trust me, if you need it down the road, you'll sure be glad it was there.

BUSINESS LIABILITY INSURANCE IS A COST OF DOING BUSINESS

Ultimately, it is up to you how much you put into your business. But the more you put into it, the more you'll get out of it. And your clients will appreciate it. They will be more likely to give their business to copywriters and freelance bloggers who have taken the time to build processes and parameters to get the job done well.

I'll be straight with you. I know several copywriters who have elected not to get business insurance. But for me, it's not an optional program, and it's not because of the threat of litigation. It's because I want to know that everything I have put into building this business will be protected in the future. I have worked so hard to get to this point. I want to protect my time, my effort, the quality of my work, and my pride.

I hope you will do the same for your business.

NOTES

MISTAKE #6
WAITING TOO LONG TO LEVERAGE THE POTENTIAL OF SOCIAL MEDIA

IN THIS CHAPTER, I want to talk about the power of social media and the mistake I made by waiting too long to develop an active presence.

I know you're probably wondering why I waited so long and how long I waited. After all, I've been in the marketing business for over 25 years and know the importance of spending time where your customers are. The answer? No good reason. I just didn't do it. And yes, I regret it.

I let myself get so caught up in the daily grind that I didn't have time to focus on social media. Rather, I didn't create the time and didn't have those boundaries in place that I do now. Plus, I had so much work coming in that I just didn't have time for much else. Even lead generation, something I talked about earlier, took a back seat— another big mistake.

When I realized the importance of establishing a social media presence, I had missed numerous opportunities to connect with potential clients, showcase my expertise, and grow my brand. This oversight taught me a valuable lesson about prioritizing social media as a fundamental aspect of modern business strategy.

Just how big of an impact was that delay in creating more of an online presence? Honestly, I'll never know. However, consider the statistics below to help drive the point home, especially if you are a new small business owner wondering how to get your products and services in front of the right people.

A 2024 article from Exploding Topics shares the following social media numbers.

- Facebook has 3.06 billion users
- YouTube has 2.70 billion subscribers
- Instagram has 2.35 billion active users
- X (formerly known as Twitter) has 600 million users
- Pinterest has 518 million active pinners (okay, not sure that's what their members are called, but I'm going to go with it)
- LinkedIn has 310 million users

Obviously, I am not listing all the platforms out there, as there are too many to count. But I have since determined that the list above includes the best possible platforms for small business owners, such as myself, to promote the products and services that we sell.

So, in all the time it took for me to "get active," I was missing out on all those people. Imagine the possibilities sitting out there that I had no clue existed. It's a bit overwhelming—and depressing—when you think about it.

THE POWER OF SOCIAL MEDIA

Now that we have discussed the size of the prize, or at least the potential of these platforms, let's get into what that means for you, the small business owner (or, in my case, me).

As of April 2024, 62.3% of the world's population used social media. With the average daily usage at 143 minutes, it's clear that people are spending a significant portion of their time on social media platforms.

Additionally, the average person engages with 6.7 different social networks per month, which means you can't put all your eggs in one basket (like I did, focusing only on LinkedIn for quite some time).

From January 2023 to January 2024, social media users worldwide grew by 320 million people. If you're paying attention, that's nearly the population of the U.S., which is just over 342 million people as of the day I am writing this chapter.

For small business owners, this means an unprecedented ability to reach a vast and varied audience. When considering your overall marketing budget, social media provides a cost-effective way to engage with customers, build brand awareness, and grow the community without spending a dime. It allows businesses to feature their products and services, share their stories—like what I am doing right now—and interact with customers in real time.

However, the risks of not being on social media are equally significant. Without a social media presence, businesses miss out on connecting with their audience where they are most active. This can lead to missed opportunities for customer engagement, brand building, and even sales. And when your business is just starting out, like mine was last year, that's a painful thought.

DEVELOPING A SOCIAL MEDIA STRATEGY FOR YOUR SMALL BUSINESS

I know first-hand how overwhelming it can be to manage your business's day-to-day operations and all the extra things you need to do to keep those leads coming in. It's a lot; the last thing you want to do is work 24/7.

But, you must find a way to make social media a part of your business. You may need to work with a third party who can take this off your plate or invest in tools that can help simplify your postings and allow you to schedule things in advance. Either way, I hate to be the bearer of bad news, but every small business owner, myself included, needs to figure out this social media game.

So, where do you start? Here are six steps to help you develop a solid social media strategy:

1. SETTING CLEAR GOALS

Start by defining your social media goals. Do you want to increase brand awareness, drive more traffic to your website, or generate leads? Having specific goals will help you focus your efforts and measure your progress.

For example, if your goal is to boost brand awareness, you might aim to increase your followers by a certain percentage each month. Below are some of my goals. They're super simple, since I am really just getting started with some of these channels, and I'll check in on them in a few months to see if it is time to set new goals.

- Get to 500 followers on Instagram (I'm still trying to crack the code on this one)

- Get to 100 followers on my Facebook business page

- Post on Instagram at least three times per week

- Post on LinkedIn at least once per week

2. IDENTIFYING YOUR TARGET AUDIENCE

Knowing your audience will help you create content that resonates with them. Consider their interests, demographics, and the problems they are trying to solve. Use tools like surveys, analytics, and customer feedback to better understand your audience.

When you know who you're talking to, you can tailor your messages to meet their needs better and build a more engaged community.

3. CHOOSING THE RIGHT PLATFORMS

Not all social media platforms are created equal. Different platforms attract different demographics and serve different purposes. For instance, LinkedIn is great for B2B connections, and this was my initial focus when I launched my business. In fact, it's still a big focus for me today because my company, Copywriting For You, is designed to write content for other businesses to help them grow website traffic. Since I am targeting a business audience, I must spend time on LinkedIn.

Instagram, however, is perfect for visual content and engaging with a younger audience. It's also a great platform for authors and book lovers to discuss books and their love of reading. I recently shared a blog post about how many writers love to read and how reading books can make us better at what we do. Now I use Instagram to discuss my business and my first book, *Perseverance. Reinvention.* I'll use it to discuss this book, too.

The key here is to choose platforms that align with your business goals and where your target audience is most active. This way, you can focus your efforts and resources on the channels that will give you the best return.

4. CREATING A CONTENT PLAN

Consistency is key in social media. I'm not going to get into this too much in this chapter because I will discuss it more in-depth in one of my subsequent chapters about another mistake (yes, the lack of a consistent posting schedule). However, here are some basic rules of the road.

- **Create a content calendar:** Plan your posts in advance to maintain consistency.

- **Mix content types:** To keep your audience engaged, use blog posts, videos, infographics, and user-generated content.

- **Provide value:** Keep your content educational, entertaining, or inspiring.

- **Save time:** A content calendar helps solo entrepreneurs manage their time efficiently by organizing posts in advance.

- **Stay flexible:** Allow room for spontaneous, timely content.

5. ENGAGEMENT AND COMMUNITY BUILDING

Social media is not just about broadcasting your message; it's about engaging with your audience. Respond to comments, participate in conversations, and show appreciation for your followers.

Building a community takes time and effort, but it's worth it. Engaged followers are more likely to become loyal customers and advocates for your brand. Always allocate time daily to interact with your audience and nurture these relationships. Remember, if you scratch their back, they'll scratch yours. Okay, that analogy might be gross, but you get my drift, right?

6. USING ANALYTICS AND ADJUSTING YOUR STRATEGY

You need to track and analyze your performance to know if your social media efforts are paying off. Use tools like Google Analytics,

Facebook Insights, and other social media analytics tools to monitor your metrics.

Look at what's working and what's not, and be ready to adjust your strategy accordingly. Consider this real example. For one week in July 2024, I set up a Facebook campaign for my first book through Ingram (a large book distributor). If you were to see the results, you might think this is pretty good. Over 31,000 impressions, 181 clicks, and a click-through rate of .57%.

But here's the bad news. It didn't result in any sales. Not one. So now I am taking the time to assess the results and see what changes I need to make for better performance next time.

Regularly reviewing your performance helps you stay on track with your goals and make informed decisions to improve your social media presence.

THE SOCIAL MEDIA PRESENCE I AM BUILDING NOW

Now that we have discussed what you should do to get started and avoid the same mistake I made, let's talk about what I am doing today. I'll admit it's still a process. As a small business owner, especially a team of one, I don't necessarily have the budget to pay someone to manage this on my behalf (though it is definitely something I am exploring).

However, I think I'm hobbling along, and the followers are starting to show up. Here's what I'm doing today:

- **Instagram:** I post two to three times weekly on Instagram to share recent blog posts, promote my book, or highlight my business services. Consistent posting helps keep my audience engaged and informed about what I'm up to. And my ultimate goal is to post once a day for maximum engagement.

- **Facebook:** I cross-post my Instagram content using Meta to my Facebook business page. This ensures that I'm reaching my audience on multiple platforms without much extra effort and keeps my messaging and branding consistent.

- **LinkedIn:** I post on LinkedIn about topics that align with a B2B audience. Sometimes, I share content on my business and personal pages to maximize reach and engagement.

- **Pinterest:** I post my blog content to Pinterest, which helps drive traffic to my website. Pinterest is great for sharing visually appealing content and attracting a broader audience.

- **Twitter:** I post my blogs and book-related content on X (Twitter), shooting for at least one post per week. This platform helps me connect with a diverse audience and join relevant conversations. Plus, I've been on Twitter since 2009 so why not keep it going?

Consistency is key. Regular posting helps build a recognizable brand and keeps your audience engaged. It also signals to social media algorithms that your account is active, which can help increase your visibility. So don't make the same mistake I did. Get on these accounts now to start growing your following and get more of the right eyeballs on your products and services.

THE MOVE TO VIDEO CONTENT

Earlier this year, I invested in vlogging equipment to create weekly content for my website. However, with my book launch in June 2024, I have used the equipment mostly for book promotion. Video content has become a powerful tool in my social media strategy. It allows me to connect with my audience more personally and provides a more memorable way to share my message.

Creating videos has helped me showcase the passion behind my work, whether it's discussing copywriting tips, sharing insights from my book, or giving a behind-the-scenes look at my business. The feedback from my audience has been positive, and I've seen increased engagement and interest in my content. Want to check out some of my videos? Take a look at my YouTube channel at https://www.youtube.com/@CopywritingForYou and subscribe. I promise there will be more great content to come.

Moving forward, I plan to balance my video content between promoting my book and providing valuable insights related to copywriting and running a small business. This approach keeps my content diverse and helps me reach different segments of my audience. And remember, you can share video content on all those channels I mentioned earlier. It's a win-win!

TIPS FOR SMALL BUSINESS SOCIAL MEDIA SUCCESS (WITHOUT GETTING OVERWHELMED)

Every business needs to get its start somewhere, and it's no different when building a social media strategy. So rather than pushing off social media altogether, find a place to start that you can manage, even if it is small. And while I hate to say that some presence is better than no presence because consistency really does matter, take the pressure off yourself and do what you can.

Here is how you can get started without getting overwhelmed and breaking the bank.

- **Start Small:** Pick one or two platforms to focus on first. Trying to be everywhere at once is a recipe for burnout. I initially started with

LinkedIn and Twitter because they made sense for my business. When I released my book, I determined that I needed a broader presence on sites such as Instagram, Facebook, and even Pinterest.

- **Use Scheduling Tools:** Tools like Buffer or Hootsuite can help you schedule posts in advance, so you're not scrambling every day. I'll be honest that I currently do most of this manually, using the embedded scheduling tools within each platform. But, if you have the means to do so, these external tools can really help.

- **Repurpose Content:** Don't reinvent the wheel. Turn a blog post into a series of social media posts, or use snippets from your videos for quick updates.

- **Batch Your Work:** Set aside a specific weekly time to create and schedule your social media content. This will keep you organized and reduce stress.

- **Engage with Your Audience:** Even if you only have a few followers, engage with them. Respond to comments and messages to build a loyal community.

- **Keep It Light:** Not every post needs to be a masterpiece. Share a funny meme, a quick tip, or a behind-the-scenes photo to keep things interesting. Just make sure it is on brand and aligns with your business.

- **Track Your Progress:** Use the analytics tools available on social media platforms to see what's working and adjust as needed. Don't stress about the numbers; focus on what you can learn.

- **Ask for Help:** If it's within your budget, consider hiring a freelancer or a social media manager to help you out. Even a few hours a week can make a big difference.

Remember, the goal is progress, not perfection. Social media is a marathon, not a sprint. Do what you can, and don't be too hard on yourself.

DON'T WAIT: START LEVERAGING SOCIAL MEDIA TODAY

Waiting too long to leverage social media's potential cost me valuable opportunities for growth and engagement. Social media is a powerful tool for connecting with your audience, building your brand, and driving business success. If you start developing a social media strategy today, you can avoid the pitfalls I experienced and set your business on a path to greater visibility and customer loyalty.

I encourage you to follow my journey on social media and stay connected. I'm sharing tips, insights, and updates regularly, and I'd love to engage with you there. Together, we can learn and grow in this digital landscape.

And now, on to my next mistake.

NOTES

MISTAKE #7
NOT POSTING REGULAR
CONTENT TO MY BLOG

IT'S FUNNY TO ME, thinking of my business as a content writer and copywriter. I literally make a living writing content for businesses to share on their websites so that they can draw in more of the right customers to buy their products or services. When I onboard new clients, they consistently ask me how often they should post, how long their blog posts should be, etc. And I always give them a recommendation.

But the truth is that I don't necessarily practice what I preach. Sometimes, I'm great at posting two or three blogs weekly on my website and then sharing those posts on social media. Other times, I let one week, two, or even three weeks go by before sharing anything. And while I am getting better at it, this is a mistake that I implore you not to make.

And so, as I continue along in this series of the top ten mistakes I made my first year, let's dip our toes into mistake # 7, which is all about not posting regular content to my blog. And, I'll take that a step further as this mistake is bigger than that. It's also about not leveraging social media to its fullest—exactly what I talked about in the previous chapter.

WHY IS POSTING CONTENT ON YOUR OWN BLOG SO IMPORTANT?

Before I get too far down the path here, I want to level just for a moment on who I think the target audience is for this particular chapter. My intended audience is new small business owners in the content creation space, specifically written content designed to inform or sell. However, I realize there is a secondary audience out there: Any small business owner trying to grow their online presence. And of course, I am targeting copywriters and content writers who are just getting started in the business.

While I am writing to other copywriters and content writers, I suspect many more readers can benefit from what I have to say. The message is this: Your website needs a steady stream of content to stay relevant. And not just any content. You need great content that shares a unique point of view and helps to solve a problem that someone might be having.

When you don't have great content, your website feels like a ghost town—quiet, a little eerie, and not where people want to hang out. Think of your blog as the heartbeat of your online presence. It's what keeps things lively and interesting. Without regular, high-quality content, your website becomes just another page in the vast sea of the internet. And let's be honest, nobody wants their website to be the online equivalent of a tumbleweed blowing through a deserted town. You need to keep things fresh. Keep things interesting. And that's what content does for your website.

IS CONTENT ONLY WRITTEN?

Here is something I have learned as a marketer over the last 25 years, especially as technology has evolved and consumer needs and preferences have changed—content comes in all forms.

While my business is in the space of content writing and copywriting, I know that there is more to it than that. Mediums like video content, infographics, podcasts, and even interactive quizzes can do wonders for your website. Think about it—sometimes, people just want to watch a quick video or glance at an infographic that breaks down a complex idea into something digestible (and maybe even fun). We live in a world where attention spans are shorter than ever, so why not give your audience something that grabs their attention and keeps them engaged?

Videos can be a fantastic way to show your brand's personality and build brand recall, whether it's a quick tip, a product demo, or even a behind-the-scenes look at your business. Infographics? They're like the Swiss Army knife of content—they look great (when done right), are fun to watch, are easy to share, and are packed with information that's easy to understand.

By mixing up your content types, you're keeping your website fresh and catering to different learning styles. I've totally embraced the video side of this over the recent months, kicking off my YouTube channel with regular content and sharing those videos on social media channels such as Instagram, Facebook, X (formerly known as Twitter... how often do we need to say this, really?), and even Pinterest. And the results have really paid off, helping to grow my followers and more interest in my products and services.

HOW MUCH CONTENT IS ENOUGH?

This all begs the question, how much content is enough? To be honest, this is a tricky question. The way I see it, you can never have too much great content. But that's the keyword: Great. What makes great content? Let's answer that question before we really dig into the frequency and cadence of content creation.

WHAT IS GREAT CONTENT?

Ask yourself this question and see how you answer it—seriously, ask yourself this question right now—what makes great content? If you're like me, you probably define great content as grabbing your attention from the get-go and not letting go. It's the kind of content that makes you want to keep reading or watching, even if you had every intention of just skimming it. Great content gives you a sense of satisfaction, yet it often leaves you wanting more, like a good book you can't put down. It's content that makes you laugh, think, or even say, "Wow, I never thought of it that way before."

Great content solves a problem or answers a question you didn't even know you had. It introduces you to new ideas, perspectives, or even products you didn't realize you needed. It's the kind of content that you're excited to share with others because you know they'll appreciate it as much as you do. In short, great content doesn't just inform—it engages, entertains, and inspires.

Here are a few key ingredients of great content:

- **Content that makes you want to keep reading or watching:** You're hooked from the first sentence and can't stop until the end.

- **Content that leaves you asking for more:** It piques your curiosity and makes you eager for the next piece.

- **Content that makes you laugh:** A little humor goes a long way in making content relatable and memorable. And does the content make you laugh out loud? Score! Honestly, this is the best content because other people might notice your laughter and ask what's so funny. This stuff makes great content go viral and is excellent for your small business and your brand.

- **Content that solves a pain point:** It addresses a problem or need and offers a solution that makes you think, "Why didn't I find this sooner?"

- **Content that introduces you to something new:** Whether it's a fresh idea, a new perspective, or a product you didn't know existed, it opens your eyes to possibilities you hadn't considered before.

CREATING GREAT CONTENT

Now that we know how to define great content, it all boils down to making it happen. This is where things get easier said than done, and I have faced my own roadblocks, especially in my first year of copywriting.

Creating great content takes time, effort, and a lot of energy, which you might not have after managing your business during a long day. But you need to make it happen, either by yourself or by bringing in a reliable third-party content creator to do this on your behalf.

While I myself am contemplating working with a third party to help augment my content, for now, I'm taking the solo path. And for a lot of small business owners, especially those in the content writing business, you're probably going to do the same. For now. Until you grow.

GETTING STARTED WITH GREAT CONTENT

So, how do you get started? Here are some tips I have learned over the last year.

- **Start with a solid plan:** Know your audience, your goals, and what you want each piece of content to achieve. It's like building a house—you need a blueprint before you start hammering nails.

- **Break it down into manageable chunks:** Writing a full blog post can feel overwhelming, so tackle it in smaller sections.

Write the intro first, then focus on one point at a time. Remember, the key to a great post is to tell them what you're going to tell them, tell them, and then tell them what you told them. Of course, make sure the content is unique, authentic, and shares something new.

- **Keep a content ideas list:** Inspiration strikes at the strangest times. Keep a list on your phone or in a notebook to jot down ideas as they come. You'll thank yourself later.

- **Batch your work:** Dedicate specific blocks of time to creating content. Whether it's a few hours each week or one full day a month, batching helps you get in the zone and be more productive.

- **Don't be afraid to revise:** Great content isn't written in one go. Step away from your draft, then come back with fresh eyes to polish and refine it.

POSTING REGULARLY: GREAT CONTENT DOESN'T MATTER IF YOU DON'T SHARE IT

Let's talk about social media again. I discussed this in my last chapter because I failed to leverage social media to its potential. Sure, I believe I have written some pretty great blog posts. But, putting them on my website alone is not enough, especially when a website is new and needs time to start indexing in Google (something my website is finally doing, thank you very much).

Okay, gloating time is over. Let's get back to the main point here. You need to do more than just post your blog to your website and hope for the best. Yes, this is where it starts, but there are more steps to take. And that takes us to social media.

I've shared this before, but current data suggests that people spend a lot of time each day on social media—143 minutes per day. So, of course, it stands to reason that if you want to reach your customers, you need to be present on social media, too. But what does that look like?

HOW OFTEN TO POST GREAT CONTENT

There are multiple schools of thought on how often you should post on each channel. And though I'll provide some best practices below, it's important to think of it from the perspective of a consumer. How often would you want to hear from the brands you love? How often do you want to hear from brands that are new to you but might have something to offer that interests you? And how much is too much? Consider these questions as you look at the following recommendations.

INSTAGRAM

Instagram is all about visuals, so focus on high-quality images, infographics, and short videos (like Reels). Ideal content includes behind-the-scenes looks, tips, and quotes that resonate with your audience. My posts tend to be about my first book, *Perseverance. Reinvention.* and general content about my favorite books, reading, and helpful tips for content writers.

Generally, I recommend one to two posts daily to keep your feed fresh and your audience engaged. Keep captions concise but interesting—think around 150 to 200 characters. Don't forget to use relevant hashtags to increase your reach, and mix in some Stories to give followers a more personal glimpse into your brand. I'll talk about hashtags more later. Hashtags were a headache for me for a while, but I finally understand why they are so important, and you should, too.

FACEBOOK

Facebook is great if you have a mix of content types, from longer-form posts to images, videos, and links. I failed to create a Facebook page right off the bat when I started my business, which I regret to this day. One of the reasons I love Facebook now is that it is a great way to share your business content with friends and family members who are interested. If they like your content, they may share it with their family members and friends, thus broadening your reach and helping you get in front of more eyeballs.

However, I seem to find many conflicting recommendations on how often to post. Hootsuite suggests posting one to two times per day, and this is probably my best recommendation as well. For me, one post per day is adequate unless something super exciting happens that I want to share with my prospective business audience. That said, I'm not sure what might come up that would require me to post two times in a day.

For quick updates, posts can be 40 to 80 characters, but you can go longer if you're sharing something more detailed, like a blog post or a video. I typically start with a brief lead-in and then share the link to one of my videos on my YouTube channel, an external article that I might find interesting, or an article on my own business blog.

As a quick tip, engaging with your audience through comments and shares is key, so be sure your content encourages interaction.

LINKEDIN

LinkedIn is the place for professional, thought-provoking content. When I started my business, I put all of my eggs in this basket, and while my content definitely got eyeballs, I quickly learned it wasn't enough. Use LinkedIn for your B2B-focused content, including tips, tricks, and how-tos that will resonate with other business professionals.

Try for one post per day with posts around 100 to 200 words.

PINTEREST

Pinterest is all about inspiration and ideas, so your content should look great and be highly shareable. That's why Pinterest is so popular for things like recipes—people tend to want to share this content with others. Currently, my infographics and blogs tend to get the most impressions. To date, my most popular Pinterest post is related to pricing copywriting and content writing services.

Pinning one post per day is ideal, and each pin should link back to valuable content on your website. Remember, the goal is to always get people to spend more time on your website, getting closer and closer to a conversion.

So keep descriptions brief but keyword-rich, around 100 characters, to help your pins get discovered. Focus on creating pins that offer solutions, tips, or ideas that your target audience is searching for, whether it's infographics, tutorials, or compelling blog post graphics.

TWITTER

Twitter—a.k.a. X—is the place for quick, snappy updates. With a limit of 280 characters per tweet, you need to be concise and engaging. While I think this is a bit excessive, many experts suggest three to four tweets per day to stay active in your followers' feeds. For me, one post a few times a week is adequate for my audience.

Share a mix of content—links to your blog posts, retweets, industry news, and even polls or questions to spark conversations. Since Twitter moves fast, make sure your content is timely and relevant, and don't be afraid to jump into trending topics when appropriate.

GETTING STARTED WITH CONTENT

I know that getting started with content can feel overwhelming, and it's a lot to take on when you have a business to run. Trust me, I'm a writer, and it's what I do all day, every day. But finding the time to develop content for my own website can sometimes fall by the wayside. Of course, that just so happens to be the point of this entire chapter—don't let the importance of developing content for your business become a bottom priority.

If you don't have the time or skills to create the content, find a business partner who can help. There are many amazing writers—like yours truly—who can help you write great content to get your content strategy off the ground.

Need help with topics? Here are some recommendations that I tend to give small business owners when we are scoping out initial projects.

- **How Your Business Got Its Start:** Share your origin story—what inspired you to start your business, the challenges you faced, and the milestones you've hit along the way. This personal touch helps your audience connect with your brand on a deeper level.

- **What to Look for in [Your Industry]:** Whether you're in real estate, retail, or dog grooming, a "what to look for" guide can help position you as an expert in your field. Plus, it's a great way to incorporate relevant keywords that your potential customers are searching for.

- **Top 5 Myths About [Your Industry]:** Busting common myths is a fantastic way to educate your audience while addressing misconceptions that could be holding them back from purchasing.

- **[Year] Trends in [Your Industry]:** People love to stay on top of trends, and this type of content keeps your blog current and positions you as a forward-thinking leader in your industry.

- **How to Get the Most Out of [Your Product/Service]:** Offering practical tips and tricks for using your product or service adds value and helps your customers see its full potential.

WHAT'S MORE IMPORTANT? BLOGS OR VIDEOS?

If you're like me when I was trying to figure all of this out, your head might be spinning as you try to figure out where to invest your content marketing dollars. Should you invest in blogs or videos? I hate to break it to you, but the answer is both.

Blogs are highly informative pieces that can help provide key information that consumers need to decide if they want your product or service. But perhaps even more important is a blog's ability to aid your search engine optimization (SEO) efforts. And then video serves as a great way to help that information consumers are consuming sink in.

So yeah, you need to do both. Start small with maybe one blog post a week, and as soon as you can, start layering in video content. You need to start somewhere. And I know what you're going to ask me now: How much is all of this going to cost?

BUDGETING FOR YOUR BLOG AND VIDEO CONTENT CREATION

The cost of a blog post can vary widely based on the writer's experience and the complexity of the topic. A 500-word article written by a beginner might cost you anywhere from $3 to $25. In contrast, more experienced writers often charge between $30 and $150 for the same word count. And if you're looking for a true expert—someone with a deep understanding of the subject matter and years of experience—you might be looking at $1,000 or more for that same 500-word blog.

When I first dipped my toes into blogging as a side hustle back in 2019, I charged just $0.04 per word. That meant a 500-word blog cost just $20. Seemed like a steal for my clients, right? And it was, especially when the content was well-crafted and SEO-optimized. As you can imagine, the work started flooding in.

When it comes to video content, you have options too. Hiring a professional, like I did with TreeTop Media, to create a background and promo video will cost more, but the investment can pay off. If you're on a tighter budget, consider purchasing some basic video equipment—a microphone kit, vlogging camera, boom stand, ring light, and portable Zoom recorder. You could get started for around $1,000 to $1,500.

Whether it's a well-written blog or engaging video content, investing in quality is key to making your content marketing efforts pay off.

P.S.: Remember those hashtags I talked about earlier? Here's the thing: They matter more than you realize, but thankfully, finding the right ones is not all that difficult. Know that hashtags help increase your posts' visibility on platforms such as Instagram and Twitter, but they can help with all social media platforms.

To find the right hashtags for your content, do a Google search to see what comes up. Scroll the platforms for similar content from other members and see their hashtags. When you use hashtags correctly, you'll grow your audience faster, which means you'll be getting your content in front of more people.

NOTES

MISTAKE #8
RELYING TOO MUCH (OR NOT ENOUGH) ON ARTIFICIAL INTELLIGENCE

NOW I AM GOING TO JUMP into a hot topic—artificial intelligence. There are so many schools of thought on this one, and it's not just on the side of the content writer.

I have clients who love using artificial intelligence tools like ChatGPT and Jasper. I have clients who absolutely forbid it. And, of course, I have clients who are open to a hybrid approach that combines human writing with augmented content from AI tools. And honestly, I don't know what the right approach is. As such, my own point of view continues to change. I am in favor of using AI for some things, and opposed to using it for others..

So, let's talk about why my first approach at using AI was a mistake and why it became such a confusing one, at that.

THE ARTIFICIAL INTELLIGENCE CONUNDRUM FOR WRITERS

I first started paying attention to the use of ChatGPT among writers in the industry when a BusinessInsider article came out. The article shared the story of a man who wrote a children's book with ChatGPT and went on to publish it. Ammaar Reshi used ChatGPT to write and illustrate the book in just 24 hours, then turned to Amazon's self-publishing platform to make it available for the world to buy.

The book, *Alice and Sparkle,* is still available today. However, the book only has an Amazon rating of 3.3, and on Goodreads, where devout readers tend to turn to for all things book-related, only a rating of 1.8.

This said, while the book is certainly not going to make Reshi a rich man, the whole thing definitely got people talking about how tools like ChatGPT can and should be used. And it's a pretty big conversation still today, one that comes up now in just about every client kick-off conversation that I have.

And what does that conversation look like?

- How do you incorporate AI tools like ChatGPT into your writing process?
- Can AI-generated content match the quality of human-written content?
- What are the potential risks of using AI tools for content creation?
- Will AI replace the need for human copywriters in the future?
- How do you balance using AI with maintaining a unique and authentic voice in my content?
- Are there specific tasks where AI is more beneficial than others?
- How do you ensure that the content produced with AI is original and not plagiarized?
- Can AI tools help with SEO optimization and keyword placement?
- What are the ethical considerations of using AI in copywriting?
- How do you handle revisions when AI-generated content doesn't meet my expectations?

CLIENTS STARTING TO DEMAND THE USE OF ARTIFICIAL INTELLIGENCE

Let's take a step back for a moment. I've been writing for a long time—since back when you had to actually thumb through an encyclopedia to find the information you needed for a research paper or an article. I've used typewriters, word processors, old-school computers, and, of course, now my beloved Apple MacBook Pro to pound out story and article after story and article.

So, when all this AI talk came about, I largely ignored it—until I couldn't. A client that I had been working with for quite some time decided to part ways with me because I wasn't willing to use AI to help write my articles. I was floored. This very same client had been praising my work for months, reaching out to me with extra work whenever he was over capacity. And I loved writing for him.

But then it was over because I wouldn't use AI? I just didn't get it. If he loved my work as a human writer, why was AI now becoming a requirement? And to make matters more confusing, his pay rate wasn't dropping, and he paid well—his per-word rate was twice what I typically charged new clients. So what was the point? Well, the answer was simple. He wanted twice as much work in the same period of time.

At that point, I had a bit of a reckoning with myself. What type of writer did I want to be? Did I want to keep writing human content? Did I want to experiment with artificial intelligence? The truth is, I didn't really know the answer. But I knew I didn't want to lose any more clients to this new technology.

And so I experimented.

MY AI EXPERIMENT: ASKING AI FOR ITS OPINION ON THE IMPACT OF ARTIFICIAL INTELLIGENCE ON HUMAN WRITERS

In January 2023, my now-husband and I were planning for our up-coming wedding that would occur in February 2023. We talked about our approach to our wedding vows, and he kept joking about using ChatGPT to write his vows for him.

So I did what I had previously refused to do and opened OpenAI on my laptop. Before I knew what I was doing, I posed a question to the chatbot. It responded with a surprisingly good response. I had asked ChatGPT about the impact of artificial intelligence on human writers.

Before I realized it, my mobile screen was rapidly filling with text. The 350 words that appeared made complete sense and were indeed original, as confirmed by a quick check on Copyscape Pro.

The chatbot explained that "artificial intelligence (AI) is increasingly being utilized across various industries, including blogging. Recently, AI-powered tools have emerged to assist human bloggers in multiple ways, from content generation to optimizing website traffic." But that wasn't all it had to say.

The chatbot continued along the lines of, "One of the biggest im-pacts of AI on bloggers is the ability to generate content automatically. AI-powered tools like GPT-3 can create blog posts, articles, and even news stories. These tools leverage natural language processing (NLP) and machine learning (ML) algorithms to analyze large datasets of text and produce new content that mirrors the style and tone."

WRITE THE VOWS!

That answer was pretty good if you ask my opinion. After I hammered out a quick article and posted it to my LinkedIn account, I walked back to the living room and told my husband to go for it and use AI to write the vows. "Let's see what happens," I told him. And at our wedding rehearsal, he read me some vows that were pretty good. The vows were the perfect concoction of his sense of humor with some grammatically correct writing.

ONTO MY GREATEST MISTAKE

I had much more faith in what AI could do at this point. The quality of the writing was good, and in the few subsequent experiments I made, I found that I could feed it what I was thinking, and it would churn out content that not only included my thoughts but added to them. And it was good, really good.

The only thing the tool couldn't do—at least not at that time—was source current statistics and figures. Since search engine optimization (SEO) requires linking to reputable external websites and your own internal content, I found an easy solution. I would go find the data and statistics that I needed for my article, would feed that and my point of view and the objective of my article into the tool, and voila—within minutes, I had an article.

It took me a fraction of the time to write an article using AI compared to writing it from scratch. The time savings were undeniable. What would typically take me a couple of hours to draft, revise, and polish now took me just a fraction of that time. With ChatGPT, I could focus more on the creative aspects of writing, such as brainstorming ideas and refining the tone, while the tool handled the bulk of the content creation.

I decided to put it into practice. After all, more and more clients were reaching out looking for writers who were familiar with using AI tools to streamline their writing. People wanted content, and they wanted it faster than ever. At that point, I felt I would miss a window of opportunity if I didn't start using it, too.

GETTING CAUGHT RED-HANDED

Okay, before we go on, let's be clear—I didn't exactly get caught red-handed with anything. But that little subtitle sure got your attention, didn't it?

Here's what really happened. I started using AI to write outlines for blog topics that I was working on. Rather than spending 30 minutes on an outline before I started with the actual writing, I could take about five minutes to frame up an outline that would guide me through the next steps. It was fantastic!

The time savings alone from these new AI-generated outlines was like a winner-winner-chicken dinner! With the amount of time I saved, I could take on at least one more article a day. So, why wouldn't I embrace the opportunity?

But, here's where things went south. As those outlines helped me increase my productivity, I asked myself what would happen if I asked AI to start writing some sections for the article for me? Could it write an intriguing and compelling introduction? Could it help write a stronger call-to-action at the end of the article? Would the writing be just as good as what I could do on my own?

I decided to jump into the world of artificial intelligence, never asking the tool to write a complete article but only to help with sections where I felt stumped, to help overcome writers' block, and to rewrite content to make sure it was original. It was going pretty well—or, at least, I thought it was going pretty well. But it really wasn't.

And thankfully, things didn't get too far along before I pushed the brakes—hard—and came to a screeching halt. Two big clients reached out with some challenging questions. One, despite my being very upfront about the use of AI, threatened litigation. The other, thankfully, simply mentioned that they did not want AI used in their content writing going forward. And that was that—it was time to think twice about using ChatGPT.

A NEW PATH FORWARD

At this point, it was time to change my approach to AI altogether. Honestly, I was feeling wishy-washy about the whole thing. Just a year and a half ago, I couldn't imagine using a writing assistant aside from a tool such as Grammarly to help me write content. Then, I let that pendulum swing and started using it almost too much.

But I was super confused. I had some clients asking me to use it—they loved the tool and the quicker turnaround time that I could offer. I had other clients who wanted 100% original content that would make its way through an AI detector with a free and clear result—something that is getting harder and harder to do even with human-written content. I had a client threaten litigation (remember to get liability insurance!), and, to this day, he won't respond to my emails or payment request (despite his website being full of AI-written content from other writers). And other clients are happy for me to take a hybrid approach.

How could there be such varying opinions out there? And how could there be so many different opinions about the March 2024 Google algorithm update which seemed to trigger the trouble?

THE POWER OF A GOOGLE ALGORITHM UPDATE

Honestly, that algorithm update was probably one of the best things that could have happened to me as a copywriter and content writer. Even though I was getting quite good at generating and augmenting content with AI—I even worked with a graphic designer to create an infographic about 15 ChatGPT words and phrases to avoid—it never felt totally right. The joy I often found in writing, even for my many business clients, was slowly fading away.

Thankfully, this update was part of Google's ongoing effort to refine its ranking systems and reduce the prevalence of low-quality, unoriginal content on Search. The focus was clear: Prioritize content that genuinely helps users while diminishing the visibility of pages created solely to game the system.

Incorporating what they learned from earlier updates, Google wanted to reduce unhelpful, poorly constructed content by 40%. The update targeted websites that existed mainly to match specific search queries without offering real value to readers. While the content I created for my clients never fell into that spammy category, it still opened my eyes to the true power of—and need for—quality SEO efforts.

By better understanding, if a page was designed for people or search engines, Google made it clear that content quality would surpass keyword stuffing and superficial SEO tactics. This was a wake-up call and a reminder of the importance of authenticity and originality in my writing.

MY CURRENT STANCE ON THE APPROPRIATE USE OF ARTIFICIAL INTELLIGENCE

Does all this mean that I don't use artificial intelligence today? No, not at all. In fact, I still use it each and every day. However, my approach is quite different from the one I took before. Here is how I use, and don't use, AI.

HOW TO USE ARTIFICIAL INTELLIGENCE AS A COPYWRITER OR CONTENT WRITER

- **To create content plans and outlines:** AI is a fantastic tool for organizing thoughts and structuring content before I begin writing.

- **To create header tags:** While I love writing paragraph after paragraph, I often have to remind myself to break content up into 300-word or fewer increments for easy reading and SEO requirements. So, ChatGPT is super helpful in creating keyword-focused header tags (your H1s, H2s, and H3s) that need to be prominent within the article.

- **To brainstorm new topics for client blogs:** When I'm stuck trying to come up with ideas, AI helps me generate fresh topics that align with my client's needs.

- **To get insights into keywords and phrases:** AI tools can quickly analyze keyword trends, giving me a solid foundation from which to work.

- **To help with geo-specific pages:** When creating multiple pages with similar content for different locations, AI assists in making each one unique enough to avoid any issues with duplicative content.

- **To clean up bullet points within blogs:** AI is great for tidying up lists and bullet points, making sure they're clear and concise.

HOW NOT TO USE ARTIFICIAL INTELLIGENCE AS A COPYWRITER OR CONTENT WRITER

Equally important to discussing how best to use AI is discussing my stance on why and when it should not be used.

- **Letting AI write a complete article:** Unless a client specifically requests it (and yes, those clients do exist), I avoid having AI generate an entire piece. Even then, I always review and edit to make sure it meets the quality standards expected by the client and myself.

- **Relying on AI for creativity:** AI can be a helpful tool, but it can't replicate the human touch needed to create engaging, original content that resonates with readers.

- **Skipping the editing process:** Even if AI helps draft parts of an article, I never skip the crucial step of human review and editing. This ensures (pun intended, as 'ensure' is a commonly overused word in AI-generated writing) that the final product is polished and professional.

- **Using AI for nuanced content:** When writing about complex or sensitive topics, I rely on my own experience and expertise rather than letting AI take the lead. This is where the opportunity to get specific insights from your client is so important—it's what allows you to write truly unique and original content from the client's point of view.

DON'T DO AI ON THE SLY

To help wrap up the learnings from this big mistake I made during my first year as a copywriter, I want to leave a couple of messages with you. First, be sure to figure out your stance on using artificial intelligence as a copywriter or content writer. No one can determine your opinion and approach other than you.

Today, my stance is to use AI for those things I mentioned above—outlines, keywords, and search terms (which are best confirmed in an SEO tool like Ahrefs or SEMRush), researching blog and article topics, and geo and location page tweaks (provided a human wrote the starting point).

And, secondly, if a client asks you about your use of ChatGPT, Jasper, or other AI tools, be truthful. I have been amazed time and again at how many clients ask me about my approach. I shared it openly and honestly, and they decided to work with me because I was upfront and didn't try to hide my approach. Apparently, many writers today are not as honest as we would hope, and that could eventually give our industry a bad name.

The important thing here is to be open and honest. Always. Simply stated, don't do AI on the sly. If a client asks you not to use it, don't use it. If you use it, make sure you are using it with good intentions in mind—not just to save time and make a quick buck. Also, invest in some tools that can help you review your work before you submit it, just to know what the tools have to say. My favorites as of the time of writing this are Originality.AI and Copyscape. Ultimately, well written content needs to stand out from other content that already exists online. It needs to be unique, offering a perspective that readers can't necessarily find elsewhere.

WRAPPING IT UP: AI IS A TOOL, NOT A SHORTCUT

Here's the thing: Mistakes are inevitable—but they don't have to be repeated. If there's one thing I've learned from my AI experiment, it's that balance is everything. AI tools can be a copywriter's best friend when used wisely, helping with tasks like creating outlines, generating ideas, and polishing up content. But, as I've learned (sometimes the hard way), they're not a substitute for the creativity, nuance, and human touch that make great writing truly stand out.

So, what's the takeaway here?

Don't let AI do all the heavy lifting. Instead, use it to lighten your load without sacrificing quality. Be transparent with your clients about how you use AI—I even mention it in my client contracts—and always put the final product through a human filter. By adopting these best practices, you can avoid the pitfalls I stumbled into and save yourself the time and energy of reinventing the wheel.

Remember, AI is a tool—use it wisely, and it'll help you become a more efficient business writer. But rely on it too much, and you might just find yourself back at square one, wondering where all the joy in writing went?

NOTES

.

MISTAKE #9
FAILING TO DEVELOP BUSINESS PARTNERSHIPS

WHEN I REFLECT ON THAT FIRST YEAR as a copywriter and content writer, I realize that aside from the writing and client management, I had no idea what I was doing. I was positive that I needed to keep my profile fresh and up to date on Upwork, and I'd be good to go. But I was so wrong.

And at this point, you know that I figured many things out the hard way. And much of it was due to my ignorance. I just thought if I had the chops to provide excellent written content to my clients, that's all I needed.

Now, to be fair, most small business owners don't build business partnerships right off the bat; this isn't necessarily something you would do in the inaugural year of business anyway. But it's something to plan for, so I felt like it was worth including in this series.

WHAT IS A BUSINESS PARTNERSHIP?

In the writing business it takes time to build a client roster, develop trust, create happy customers, and then put together that portfolio. For that reason, business partnerships aren't necessarily going to come flying in.

But, as I said before, you need to plan for this. Without great business partners, you may lose out on a highly valuable and profitable business stream. And I'm not just talking about those partners that will pay you referral commissions. Of course, it's a nice-to-have and definitely something to add to your business bucket list, but for now, let's focus on the partnerships that add value to your clients.

When you put your clients' needs first, you create convenience for them, and they'll be more likely to bring you new work. Why? You are saving them time and money by providing connections and recommendations that they don't have to keep hunting for on their own.

Consider this scenario—you're having coffee with a prospective client who wants to hire you to write a blog for them on a weekly basis. Awesome! This is excellent news. But then you go to their website, and it's awful. The site takes forever to load, the imagery is blurry and outdated, and the content is bad. Really, really bad. So what do you do?

As a writer, do you really want to create fantastic content for your clients only to direct readers to a poor website experience? Of course not. What would happen if you pass your client over to one of your business partners who can work some magic behind the scenes to fix all that technical SEO stuff and improve the user experience? Your client will love you for it!

THE BEST BUSINESS PARTNERS FOR BUSINESS WRITERS

Okay, so you want to know what business partners you should entertain for your business. And really, the world is your oyster. You can develop as many business partners as you want. But I advise you to start where you can add the most value to your clients. Think about it from the perspective of what your client needs to do to make sure that the content you write for them will give them the most bang for the buck.

I suggest you start here. Establishing these five partnerships will grow your credibility with your current and future clients. Trust me on this.

1. SOCIAL MEDIA AGENCY

Social media is non-negotiable for businesses, especially when people are spending 143 minutes a day on social media. Imagine that—143 minutes per day! I'm in the content business and can't imagine spending that much time on social platforms.

Partnering with a social media agency allows you to offer clients more than just written content—you're helping them engage with their audience, build brand awareness, and drive traffic to their site. And, if you are writing blogs for businesses, they should be sharing that content on their social media channels. This is a win-win for you and your clients.

So, what should you look for in a creative partner? Here's my take and it's really quite simple.

- **Creativity:** Can they craft engaging, relevant posts?
- **Analytical Skills:** Are they data-driven and capable of measuring success?
- **Reliability:** Will they consistently meet deadlines and maintain a regular posting schedule?

2. SEO AND WEBSITE DEVELOPMENT AGENCY

Your written content is only as good as the website it lives on. Partnering with an SEO and website development agency makes sure that your clients' websites look great and are also optimized for search engines.

This way, the great content you create has the best chance of being found and appreciated by the target audience. When your client sees their content rising to the top of search engine results pages, they're more likely to hire you for more and more.

What to Look For in an SEO and website development agency:

- **Technical Expertise:** Do they understand both front-end and back-end development?

- **SEO Knowledge:** Are they up to date with the latest SEO practices?

- **User Experience Focus:** Can they create a website that's easy to navigate and fast to load?

3. FRACTIONAL CMO

Some of your clients might have the resources to tackle marketing tactics but don't know how to develop a cohesive strategy. This is where a fractional Chief Marketing Officer (CMO) can be invaluable. Fractional CMOs are becoming increasingly popular for companies that don't have the funds to allocate to a full-time resource.

If this concept is a bit unfamiliar to you, basically a fractional CMO is a marketing executive who works with a company on a part-time or contract basis, offering the expertise of a Chief Marketing Officer without the commitment or cost of a full-time hire.

Unlike a traditional CMO, who is deeply embedded in the organization's day-to-day operations, a fractional CMO typically focuses on high-level strategy, guiding the company's marketing direction, and overseeing key initiatives for a set period or project. This arrangement works well for businesses that need expert leadership to drive marketing efforts but don't require—or can't justify—the resources for a permanent CMO.

These professionals can help your clients develop a marketing plan that aligns with their business goals. And then your content becomes that much more effective.

Here's what to look for in a fractional CMO.

- **Strategic Thinking:** Can they see the big picture and guide long-term planning?

- **Industry Experience:** Do they have a proven track record in your client's industry?

- **Communication Skills:** Can they translate complex marketing strategies into actionable steps?

Beware of this one, however. There are many people out there in the remote workforce who call themselves fractional CMOs but really don't have the street credibility to do so. Be sure to do your homework and avoid imposter fractional CMOs.

5. GRAPHIC DESIGNER

As you know, I have been using the Upwork platform for quite some time to help with lead generation and introductions to prospective clients. When scrolling through potential gig opportunities, I am always surprised by how many clients are looking for someone who can both write content and create graphics to support the written content.

Yes, some writers can do this. But in most cases, this is an entirely different skill set. Trust me, you don't want me to try to create visuals for you. I promise it would be a very bad investment. Your clients will appreciate it if you have a graphic design partner who can manage that part of the project. And this means you can win more gigs.

What to look for in a graphic designer partner:

- **Creativity:** Do they have a strong portfolio that depicts their design skills?

- **Versatility:** Can they work across different mediums and styles?

- **Collaboration:** Are they open to feedback and able to work seamlessly with your writing?

5. VIDEO PRODUCTION SPECIALIST

While written content is super important and will always be needed, adding video content to a marketing strategy is where it's at. Many clients have no idea how to find a great video specialist who can provide them with high-quality videos to help them promote their business.

As video content continues to dominate online platforms, having a video production specialist as a partner can really up your game. They can help your clients create engaging video content that complements your written work. And remember, video content can create a serious lift in email click-through rates to 300%. Your clients may also see an 80% increase in conversion rates when videos are used on a landing page. And, if that doesn't sell you on the need for a video partner, consider that an estimated 64% of consumers purchase after viewing a video. Those are some pretty powerful stats if you ask me.

And if you're wondering, here's the three primary things to look for in a video production partner.

- **Technical Proficiency:** Do they have the right equipment and editing skills?

- **Storytelling Ability:** Can they turn concepts into compelling visual narratives?

- **Adaptability:** Can they produce different types of videos, from promotional clips to explainer videos?

HOW TO GET THE BEST BUSINESS PARTNERS FOR YOUR WRITING BUSINESS

Now that you know the types of partners you want for your writing business, let's talk about how to get them in the first place. The guidance I'm about to give you may surprise you: Getting great business partners starts with you, not them.

Here's why.

Just like you don't want to partner with someone who walks a good walk and talks a good talk but can't deliver, they don't want that either. You need to prove that you are as good at what you do as you say you are. This is exactly why you likely won't be able to get those partners right away in that first year of business. It takes time.

You need to build up a clientele. You probably need some bylined gigs and ghost-writing gigs that likely comprise most of your business. People need to see your work in multiple places, not just on your website. So, here's what to do to build that street credibility.

GET BYLINED GIGS

Getting your name attached to your work is like getting a golden ticket in the writing world. Bylined gigs are the ones that say, "Hey, look at me, I actually wrote this!" They give you credibility and visibility that ghostwriting simply can't. I was fortunate when I first got going in the writing space to have the opportunity to write bylined work for big sites such as FinImpact, Healthday, and Host Advice.

Start by pitching to smaller publications or niche blogs in your field. Don't be afraid to contact editors or even start with guest posts. The more bylined work you have, the easier it will be for potential partners to see you as a legitimate player in the writing game.

Here are the tactics I suggest.

- **Start Small:** Target smaller blogs or publications first.

- **Pitch Regularly:** Consistent pitching increases your chances of landing bylined work.

- **Show Off Your Bylines:** Add these pieces to your portfolio and share them on social media.

ASK FOR REVIEWS

Reviews are like gold stars for your business. But here's the thing—they don't magically appear. You have to ask for them. Start by setting up a Google Business Profile if you don't have one already. This gives potential clients an easy way to find you and read what others have to say about your work. Then, make it a habit to ask satisfied clients for reviews. The key is to make it easy for them—send a quick email with a direct link to your profile and a polite request.

Try these tactics.

- **Create a Google Business Profile:** It's free and gives your business more visibility.

- **Make the Ask:** Don't be shy—most happy clients will leave a review if you ask.

- **Follow Up:** If someone promises a review but doesn't deliver, a gentle reminder can go a long way.

ASK CLIENTS FOR TESTIMONIALS

So, before I get into this one, let me clarify that reviews and testimonials are not the same, though many people use the phrasing interchangeably. The key difference here is that you go out and ask for testimonials, usually to share them on your website and other marketing materials. You can see examples of testimonials for my business on the bottom of the homepage on my website.

Testimonials are powerful because they're like little endorsements from real people who have worked with you. Don't wait for clients to offer them—be proactive. Ask your happiest clients for a few sentences highlighting what they liked about your work. Then, display these testimonials in a big way on your website, social media, and even in your email signature if you like.

Here's what to do.

- **Be Specific:** Ask clients to focus on particular aspects of your work.

- **Make it Easy:** Provide a template or specific questions to guide them.

- **Show off Your Testimonials:** Display them on your website, proposals, and social media.

AUTHOR GUEST POSTS

Guest posting is like the handshake of the internet—it's a great way to introduce yourself and your business to a new audience. Not only does it give you bylined work, but it also helps with your SEO by creating valuable backlinks to your website.

Plus, it positions you as an expert in your field, which is exactly what potential partners want to see. When writing guest posts, aim for high-quality content that offers real value to the audience. When I first started writing guest posts to link back to my site, I worked with sites such as Copywriter Collective and Blog Herald (for the latter, I actually worked with the site to create a backlink to my site in their existing content).

Do this and see how it works for you.

- **Target Relevant Blogs:** Choose sites that align with your niche.
- **Include a Link:** Make sure your post includes a link back to your site.
- **Repurpose Content:** Use the guest post to fuel your own blog or social media channels.

SEEK OUT PRESS AND PUBLICATION OPPORTUNITIES

Last but not least, one of the best ways to gain visibility and credibility is by seeking out press opportunities, like interviews and podcasts. Getting featured in the media can position you as an expert in your field and put your name in front of a wider audience.

Start by contacting industry-related podcasts or online publications that interview professionals in your niche. Being a guest on a podcast or being interviewed for an article highlights your expertise and helps you build your brand and connect with new audiences. I've had great luck with media sites such as CanvasRebel, VoyageMinnesota, and BOLD Journey. I've even invested marketing dollars to be featured on sites such as Women's Herald, NY Weekly, and in a pretty cool article about the "Top 20 Women Leaders To Look Out For In 2024."

I have also jumped on the opportunity to participate in podcasts. I have been featured on Time For You and Ask a Fractional. I'm looking for more podcast opportunities, so if you know any, send them my way! It takes an army, right?

Here's how to find press opportunities.

- **Identify Relevant Opportunities:** Look for podcasts, blogs, or online magazines that focus on your industry.

- **Pitch Yourself:** Craft a compelling pitch that explains why you'd be a great guest or interviewee.

- **Leverage Exposure:** Share the interview or podcast episode on your website and social media to maximize the visibility and credibility it brings.

PROMOTING YOUR BUSINESS PARTNERSHIPS

Before we wrap up this mistake and my failure to develop business relationships sooner than I did, here are a few things to consider before you get too far along:

- **Review Their Portfolio:** Check out the work your potential partner has done. Is it up to the standard you would expect? Does it align with the quality you deliver?

- **Look at Their Reviews:** Just like you ask for client reviews, see what others are saying about your potential partner. Are their clients raving about them, or are there red flags?

- **Assess Their Online Presence:** How do they promote themselves? Are they active on social media, and do they portray their work effectively? This can give you insight into how they might promote your partnership.

- **Ask for References:** Don't be afraid to ask them for a couple of client references. A good partner will be happy to share.

- **Test a Small Project:** Consider working with your prospective business partner on a joint project to test the water.

- **Mention in Networking Events:** Bring up your partnerships during networking events and discussions to demonstrate the breadth of services you can offer.

- **Add to Your Email Signature:** While I don't love this idea, I have seen other writers include a brief mention or link to their partnerships in their email signatures. This might resonate with you, and if so, go for it!

- **Collaborate on Content:** You're a writer, so work with your partners on joint blog posts, webinars, or podcasts to cross-promote your services and reach a wider audience.

- **Use Testimonials:** If your partners are willing, include their testimonials about your collaboration on your website and marketing materials to reinforce the strength of your relationship.

BREAKING UP WITH A BAD BUSINESS PARTNER

Okay, I'll be honest. I really debated talking about this but decided to share some words. Sometimes, you make a bad partnership decision. I've done it, too, and have been faced with cleaning up the mess of my mistake. No, I'm not going to talk about this as Mistake #10, but I will tell you this—if things aren't going well, you need to take action. The last thing you want is to have a business partner that isn't cutting it. This can threaten your business reputation and work against you—big time.

Here's what to do:

- **Share Your Concerns:** Have an open conversation with your partner, explaining the issues and allowing them to resolve the situation.

- **Set a Time Limit:** Make the resolution time-bound so the situation doesn't drag on indefinitely.

- **Probationary Period:** If they resolve the issues, treat the next few weeks as a probationary period to see if things improve.

- **If Issues Persist:** If the problems reoccur or aren't resolved, it's time to consider ending the partnership.

- **Quit While the Going is Good:** Don't wait until things get worse—act quickly to protect your business and reputation. The longer you wait, the more damage you can do.

I've learned much about business partnerships over the last year and a half since starting my business in March 2023. I'm currently looking for some new partners, and I am planning to cut my losses on another. It's part of the business. However, when you take the time to develop relationships, it can really help your business grow. So don't hesitate to start looking for the right business partners for you.

NOTES

MISTAKE #10
NOT STARTING MY BUSINESS SOONER

FOR MANY PEOPLE, putting things off is second nature. We're always waiting for that perfect timing—going back to school, getting married, having kids, buying a house, and even starting a business.

Since starting my business, I get asked some form of the same question all the time: What took you so long? Why didn't you do it sooner? And honestly, my answer was always that the stars had not yet aligned. A reason always kept me from pursuing my dream of being a full-time writer.

I didn't think I had the chops to manage my own business. I didn't have confidence in my ability to be my own boss. There was the fear that I couldn't offset the income I was bringing in through more traditional employment. I always had a reason why I couldn't do it.

While it is true that the stars finally did align for me and the perfect timing came for me to start my business—it practically fell in my lap—I want to caution people that if they wait too long, they might miss a golden opportunity. Why? Because I firmly believe that people are meant to live out their dreams. And what's the worst thing that can happen? Do we fail? Yes, that's a risk. But we won't know until we try.

WHY WE PUSH OFF OUR DREAMS: IT'S A PSYCHOLOGY THING

Many people fail to pursue their dreams because they are afraid of failure. And yes, that fear lived and breathed in me. But honestly, it wasn't the all-consuming barrier that kept me from doing what I really wanted to do all the time—write (and read a great book now and again for good measure). The biggest obstacle that got in my way was the fear that I wouldn't generate the needed income. I wouldn't bring in the money that my family had come to rely on.

So instead of trying things on for size, I kept my passion for writing in the background. When Experian, one of the three credit bureaus in the U.S. and the company I worked for from 2012 to 2015, started a blog, I signed up to be a contributor. When Sutherland Global Services, the company I worked for from 2015 to 2018, needed content rewritten—I took the challenge head-on. Of course, it wasn't all that challenging when I was responsible for industry marketing, and we needed content to share.

When I worked for a small online lender from 2019 to 2023, my favorite part of the work was writing blogs or overseeing the creation of blogs for the company's external website. I found a way to live in my happy space, even though I wasn't doing it daily.

The challenge was that the longer I kept myself from doing what I loved to do, the unhappier I became in my career. When you find yourself doing a job you don't love, no matter how good you may be, you do yourself and everyone around you a disservice. And trust me, all the money in the world isn't going to give you the happiness that you can find when you get to do what you love to do every day.

But why do we let these fears hold us back? What is it that keeps so many of us from diving into what we're passionate about? It often comes down to a mix of psychological reasons that can quietly convince us to stay put. If this sounds like you, take a look at some of these common mental roadblocks that might be standing in your way.

I know I hit on some of these earlier, but humor me while I organize and lay it all out on the table.

- **Fear of Failure:** This is probably the biggest one. We worry about what happens if things don't work out, and that fear can paralyze us into inaction. And, while I know I talk about this a lot in my blog on my business website, Copywriting For You, there is a sad reality out there—20% of businesses fail in their first year. Perhaps even more alarming is that only half of businesses still stand after five years.

- **Comfort in Familiarity:** Even if you're not entirely happy, the comfort of what you know can keep you from leaping into something new and uncertain. But I warn you, getting too comfortable can lead to complacency and that can lead to stagnation, which is not good.

- **Imposter Syndrome:** The nagging feeling that you're not good enough or that you're just faking it can make you doubt your abilities, even when you're fully capable. Honestly, I've had a pretty successful career. I had made my first million by 2010, which I think is pretty impressive considering I didn't graduate from college until 1998. And I've hit that million-dollar mark a few more times since then—something I am quite proud of. This isn't meant to be a "wow, look at me" exclamation by any means. Rather, it's almost my way of saying to myself that I'm no imposter. When I put my mind to things, I'm good at it.

- **Lack of Resources:** Whether it's time, money, or skills, believing that you don't have what it takes to succeed can stop you before you even start. But if you want to start a writing business, all you need is a notebook, pen, and a really good laptop.

- **Overthinking:** Sometimes, we get so caught up in analyzing every possible outcome that we talk ourselves out of taking any action at all. I have discussed the concept of analysis paralysis before in the context of endless client revisions in one of my blogs, but it applies here, too. I found myself so caught up in all the reasons that starting my business wouldn't work that I forgot to think of all the reasons it would.

- **Fear of Judgment:** Worrying about what others might think if you fail—or even if you succeed—can be a major barrier. In my case, a bit of fuel was added to the fire based on the income expectations that my former spouse seemed to have. He was a chronic spender, always looking to buy the next thing. As such, I feared disappointing him. Before I knew it, I found myself pushing aside my own career dreams and instead looking for bigger and better incomes to help fund his passions, rather than my own.

- **Procrastination:** Putting things off because the task seems too big or waiting for the "right" moment can indefinitely delay your dreams. For me, my procrastination consisted of all the things earlier in this list. I let those things hold me back, thus pushing out the opportunity further and further.

THE COST OF WAITING

So, what's the risk of waiting? What is the actual cost of doing so? No, this is not meant to be a financial computation, though you can certainly do the math if you want to. The real cost of waiting is about more than just dollars and cents. It's about the missed opportunities that could have helped you grow, both personally and professionally. By waiting until January 2023 to finally make the leap and turn my side hustle into a full-time gig, I lost valuable time that could have been spent building my brand, expanding my network, and honing my skills in a highly competitive industry.

Everyone is vying for attention in the content writing space, and starting sooner could have given me a head start in growing my social media presence and establishing my name as a go-to writer. The earlier you jump in—not just get your feet wet—the more time you have to create connections, gather testimonials, and show the world what you're capable of. Trust me, there's plenty of room for talented writers, but it takes time to carve out your space.

Then there's the regret factor. Sure, the risk of failure is real—anyone who's started a business will tell you that. But compare that to the regret of never trying at all. What if you wait too long and miss out on the chance to do something amazing? The long-term consequences of inaction can weigh heavier than any potential failure. You don't want to look back and wonder, "What if I had just started sooner?"

And okay, let's talk about the money because there is a financial risk beyond those emotional and mental costs. Delaying your start can also delay your financial independence. Every month you wait is another month of not earning what you could be if you were all in. It's another month of not building the financial security of running a successful business. I'm not one of those content writers or copywriters who earn less than $100,000 per year. I'm good at what I do. I put my all into my work, and my compensation shows it.

Plus, starting earlier means more time to navigate the ups and downs, learn from your mistakes, and eventually reach a point where your business is prosperous. The longer you wait to "dive in," the more doubt or exhaustion will build up, causing the transition to be so much more difficult. Why do that to yourself?

In short, the cost of waiting is high. The lost time, missed opportunities, and lingering what-ifs can hold you back from reaching your full potential. So, if you're on the fence, consider this your nudge to start sooner rather than later.

THE REALITIES OF STARTING A BUSINESS

Starting a business isn't easy, and you've probably seen that firsthand. My goal has always been to share what I've learned so you can avoid the same pitfalls I encountered.

From the beginning, I made some rookie mistakes that cost me time, money, and a lot of stress. For instance, going cheap on a website left me with a design that didn't represent my brand well. Not having clients sign a statement of work led to misunderstandings and unpaid invoices. Undervaluing my services hurt my bottom line, while not dedicating enough time to lead generation made finding clients more challenging—and hurt my pocketbook a bit in the process.

I also neglected to protect my business with liability insurance, which was a risk I shouldn't have taken. Waiting too long to embrace social media meant I missed out on opportunities to build my audience. And let's not forget the importance of regularly updating my blog—something I didn't prioritize early on. Then there's the balancing act with AI: relying too much or too little on it can both be a problem. Finally, I underestimated the power of business partnerships, which could have helped me grow faster and get in front of more of the right people.

These lessons were hard-earned, but they've shaped my business today, and I hope they help you build yours even better. Because, yes, building a business is a lot of work. It takes dedication and perseverance. You'll give up some free time. You'll need to establish some boundaries. But it is possible. And you can absolutely be successful.

TURNING YOUR DREAMS INTO YOUR REALITY

How do you turn your dreams into reality? It all starts with setting reasonable dreams. Of course, we all want to win the lottery. Imagine those millions of dollars and all the doors it can open—a house up in the mountains or on the beach—maybe both. Never worrying about making ends meet. Moving on from being one of the 66% of Americans who live paycheck to paycheck and possibly becoming one of America's elite.

Winning the lottery has a probability of one in three million. Considering the U.S. population is just under 346 million at the time of this writing, you can see that this is just one of those dreams that might not become a reality. And while all you need to do is buy a ticket, the chances that you will get those numbers right on the right day are just not that high.

Going after a small business dream, on the other hand, is far more realistic. It's achievable. And typically, the only thing getting in your way is yourself. All those reasons I laid on the table earlier in this chapter keep you from getting off the couch and getting started.

Do you think those who win marathons, or our Olympians, simply got up one day and said they would win a medal and just made it happen? Of course not. They worked for it. They trained for it. They did their homework. And, most importantly, they owned their dream to make it a reality.

You can do this, too. But if you keep pushing it off repeatedly, it will never happen.

GETTING STARTED AND MAKING IT HAPPEN

Deciding to get started is where it all begins. But what do you do once you decide you want to get into the copywriting business? You may already be panicking. How are you going to find customers? How are you going to make sure those leads start coming in? Can you charge what you are worth, and more importantly, what rate should you start at?

You'll have a lot of questions. And up front, you won't have all the answers. One of the most beautiful things about the writing business is that you always learn. So, anticipate that you will learn a lot during your first several months. I've been writing as a side hustle since 2019, and I've been doing this full-time since the beginning of 2023. I can honestly tell you that I learn each and every day. I am constantly refining my approaches to managing my business to see what works and what doesn't. You will, too.

With an open mind and a willingness to learn—and make mistakes—you'll be well-positioned for success. That said, here is what I suggest you do to get started. It worked for me, and with some perseverance, I think it can work for you, too.

DECIDE WHAT KIND OF WRITER YOU WANT TO BE

Take some time to think about what type of writing excites you the most. Are you drawn to creating persuasive copy for sales pages, crafting engaging blog posts, or developing technical content? Knowing your niche will help you focus your efforts and attract the right clients.

What kind of writing do I do? Well, my passion is writing informative content—blogs and articles—for business websites. I write in both the B2B and B2C space, and I love the variety that this affords me. And while my business might be called Copywriting For You, the truth is that I spend most of my time content writing and less time copywriting. Why is that? It's because many clients come to me for copywriting, and we get those web pages completed. Then, they need ongoing content to help keep their website fresh and to help them rank higher in search engine page results. So, the copywriting lands the deal, but the content writing keeps that writing relationship going. It's just what I enjoy doing most, and my clients know it, so that's the work they throw my way.

START SMALL AND BUILD YOUR PORTFOLIO

Begin by taking on small projects to build a portfolio. Don't worry if they aren't high-paying gigs at first—getting experience and having samples to showcase your skills matters. I'm a big fan of the Upwork platform to help you get your start. Thousands of projects are out there just waiting for the right freelancer. And that freelancer could be you.

But Upwork isn't your only option. You can find similar gigs on Fiverr and market yourself on LinkedIn, too. You just need to find what works for you. There are plenty of email newsletters you can sign up for to give you a heads-up on companies looking for freelance writers.

SET UP YOUR BUSINESS STRUCTURE

Decide if you want to operate as a sole proprietor, LLC, or another business structure. Based on guidance from my accountant, I went with the S-corporation option. Each structure has pros and cons, so it's worth researching or consulting with a professional to see what's best for you.

To that end, I suggest you get set up with an accountant before you get too far. Their advice is worth its weight in gold and can keep you out of trouble down the road.

CREATE A PROFESSIONAL WEBSITE

You guessed it—you need a winning website, and you can not do this cheaply unless you have website development and design experience. Your website is your online business card. Make sure it reflects your brand and showcases your work. Include a portfolio section, an 'About Me' page, and clear contact information. If you're not tech-savvy—like me—investing in a good website designer can make a big difference.

ESTABLISH YOUR RATES

Pricing can be tricky, but you need to start somewhere. Research industry standards, consider your experience, and set rates that you're comfortable with. Remember, raising your rates later is easier than lowering them. Keep in mind, too, that if you stick to copywriting, you may be able to charge a higher rate than for content writing. Sales writing is designed to convert. As such, clients should be willing to part with the dollars that are spent to help them drive those conversions.

DEVELOP A MARKETING PLAN

Think about how you'll attract clients. This might include networking, social media marketing, email outreach, or even paid ads. Choose strategies that fit your budget and skills, and be consistent with your efforts. Don't delay this. You need to start promoting yourself right away.

START BUILDING RELATIONSHIPS

Networking is key in this business. Reach out to other writers, join online communities, and connect with potential clients. Look for networking opportunities in your community. Consider joining your local Chamber of Commerce to make some business connections. Building genuine relationships can lead to referrals and repeat business.

KEEP LEARNING AND IMPROVING

The writing industry is always evolving, so make it a habit to keep learning. This could be through taking online courses, reading industry blogs, or experimenting with new types of content. Coursera and Udemy offer copywriting courses that can help refresh your skills and get your head in the game.

STAY ORGANIZED

Staying organized is crucial for running a smooth operation, from managing deadlines to tracking invoices. Use tools like project management software, time trackers, and accounting apps to keep everything in order. Avoid relying on spreadsheets wherever possible. Trust me on this: multiple spreadsheets can become quite the headache come tax time.

DON'T BE AFRAID TO MAKE MISTAKES

Mistakes are part of the learning process. Don't be too hard on yourself if things don't go perfectly, initially. Learn from each experience, and use that knowledge to refine your approach as you go. Perseverance and persistence are where it's at.

WANT TO TALK TO SOMEONE WHO'S BEEN DOWN THE ROAD YOU ARE TRAVELING?

By now, you get my point—don't delay pursuing your passion. If you have a talent that the world can benefit from, you're doing everyone a disservice by not getting it out there. And the truth is that life is short. Why spend time doing something you don't love when you can do what you do love?

Starting a business isn't easy, and you've seen that firsthand. My goal has always been to share what I've learned so you can avoid the same pitfalls I encountered. These lessons were hard-earned, but they've shaped my business today, and I hope they help you build yours even better. Because, yes, building a business is a lot of work. It takes dedication and perseverance. You'll give up some free time. You'll need to establish some boundaries. But it is possible. And you can absolutely be successful.

NOTES

LESSONS LEARNED:
TURNING MISTAKES
INTO MASTERY

WHEN I THINK BACK on these last two years since starting my business, I feel a sense of awe and accomplishment. Yes, I made so many mistakes—far more than the ten I have told you about in this book. But I have also created quite a successful business.

I think part of the reason for this is I didn't let those mistakes stop me. I didn't let the client who never paid me after I rewrote his work keep me from taking on new clients. And I didn't let those weeks where I didn't hit my revenue target slow me down—yes, I have a daily and weekly revenue target.

Instead, I took those opportunities to get better. To perfect my skills as a small business owner. To become a stronger writer. And I'm super happy with where I am today.

However, I know that my mistakes might not be the same as your mistakes. In fact, if you are reading this book or have followed along with the Copywriting For You blog over the last couple of years, I hope that you used some of my mistakes as a checklist of things for you to address. That said, there are so many other mistakes out there that we can make. And these, too, can be amazing lessons that we can take and turn into something good.

But just how do we do that? Well, by no means am I a teacher. I wouldn't even call myself an expert—is anyone really an expert in this space these days when consumer needs and preferences are changing and companies are evolving everywhere we look? But I am a lifelong learner. So, I have some thoughts that might help you.

WHAT'S A GROWTH MINDSET?

The business world is full of all these buzzwords—synergy, leverage, pivot (even before the best *Friends* episode ever), low-hanging fruit, deep dive, customer-centric, disruptive innovation, elevator pitch—oh, how I could go on and on. And yes, one of those buzzwords today is the growth mindset. But this one holds some deeper meaning that can be valuable to us both personally and professionally.

A growth mindset is all about believing that our abilities and intelligence can be developed through dedication, hard work, and learning from our experiences—especially the tough ones. Instead of seeing failure as the end of the road, it becomes a stepping stone. When I realized I wasn't charging enough for my talent or the value of my deliverables, I could've just felt defeated. Instead, I took that as an opportunity to refine my pricing strategy, learn what my work was really worth, and adjust. After getting burned by a non-paying client, I decided it was time to protect myself, so I put a statement of work and MSA in place—no more guessing games about payment terms.

So, here's the thing: Setbacks are going to happen. But they don't have to keep us stuck. Take every mistake as an opportunity to reflect on your own experiences. Adapt your growth mindset. What can you learn? How can you shift from frustration to growth and become stronger on the other side?

PUTTING BOUNDARIES INTO PLACE

Let's talk a bit about boundaries. And while we're at it, let's talk about barriers. I didn't talk about this as one of my top ten mistakes because, in this case, it wasn't a mistake that I uncovered. Instead, it was this eureka moment that I stumbled upon one day when I realized that I am truly in charge of my destiny—at least as far as my business goes.

Here's the backstory. When I started writing full-time and left the corporate world, I would see a client's name pop up on my phone and would answer the call right as it came in. I would answer emails at all times of the day. And I realized that those calls were eating away at my productivity. By the time I ended the phone call, I found it challenging to get back into the groove of whatever project I had been working on when I picked up the phone.

This was truly a disservice to my clients and to me. These interruptions would literally bring my flow of words to a screeching halt, and whatever I might have been thinking should come next would evaporate from my brain. It was a shame, really.

I thought I needed to be available whenever my clients needed me. If they needed to wait for me to call back or answer the email, they might move on to a writer who would respond sooner. And then I realized something: Would a client really move on to someone else if I didn't return their call for a few hours or if I didn't respond to their email immediately?

Of course not. Further, if they were a client that expected me to be at their beck and call, it probably wasn't the best fit. So I decided to establish some boundaries. These boundaries are not barriers, however. There's a big difference.

Boundaries are healthy guidelines that protect your time and energy, while barriers are walls that shut people out entirely. Setting boundaries doesn't mean cutting people off, but instead it means creating space to do your best work. I set a clear boundary for client calls when I realized my productivity was taking a hit from constant interruptions.

Now, unless there's an emergency—which is rare in copywriting—I schedule calls in advance and take them on Tuesdays and Thursdays. This structure helps me maintain focus and gives my clients the attention they deserve during our conversations.

Setting boundaries is about more than just phone calls, though. It's also about having solid contracts in place with clear payment terms, revision limits, and timelines. I learned the hard way that if a client doesn't respect those terms upfront, it's a red flag. Clear, upfront communication is super important to avoid misunderstandings. A well-thought-out client brief that asks the right questions upfront saves time and prevents projects from veering off track.

And if a client still doesn't respect those boundaries, it's a sign they're probably not a great fit for your business. It's better to let them go and focus on clients who value your work and your time.

MASTERING TIME MANAGEMENT

This is a big one—time management. When you're self-employed, especially in this industry, it can be so easy to let time get away from you. Before you know it, you're telling your family that you are going to have to work a few nights during the week to stay on top of your backlog. Or you find that you dawdled too much during the day on social media and, before you know it, an hour has slipped away, and you need to race to catch up.

When you work for yourself, there is no one to hold yourself accountable but you. When I talk to other writers, they tell me that this can be one of the biggest things that keeps them up at night—literally and figuratively.

Though I am going to tell you how I manage my time, I want my readers to understand that you might need a different approach to time management. That's the beauty of human nature, right? What makes one person tick might not be the same for someone else. And so is the case with time management.

The key here is to find what does work for you. Try some different approaches. Know that things might ebb and flow from day to day, and that's okay, too. But try to put some structure in place to protect your work-life balance (something I'll talk about next) and to keep yourself from going crazy.

Here's what I do.

I'm not a morning person. Let's start there. This is probably the biggest thing I needed to learn—and accept—about myself when I started my business. The truth is that I don't work traditional hours. I work nights. I work weekends. But I don't do mornings.

And because I don't do mornings, I need to be super structured so that I don't let my work consistently interfere with my family life. Even though my family knows that some of my most productive writing time is in the evenings, I can't make that an everyday thing. It's not good for me or my health. And it's not good for my marriage. If you read my first book, *Perseverance. Reinvention.* then you know how important it is to me to set healthy boundaries in our relationship and to find that time to come together.

I start writing sometime between 10 and 11 each morning. Some mornings, I hit the downstairs home gym—not nearly as fancy as I made that sound—for a workout after I wake up. On other days, I go for a walk to clear my mind. Sometimes, I simply enjoy sipping my coffee and scrolling through social media to catch up on the latest buzz. (We all know that social media is where all the "important" stuff is happening—just kidding, kind of). Once I've taken a moment for myself, it's time to get into my work.

Each day, I have a revenue target in mind—a specific amount of work I need to complete to reach my income goals. While I won't share that exact number with you, let's just say it's a stretch goal, but it's achievable if I stay on top of my lead generation. In addition to client work, I also block out time for social media management. Meta has tools that make it easy to stay consistent with my posting goals for both Facebook and Instagram. I also set aside time to create content for my blog, which helps with lead generation and, of course, work on my books. By the time this book is in your hands, I'll already be deep into my third book (but the topic is still a surprise. Unless you know me personally and know that I'm not good at keeping that kind of secret).

The key is structuring your day around your personal rhythm and goals. For me, it's all about balance—finding time for productivity, creativity, and a little bit of scrolling. That way, I can stay on track without burning out, and I know my targets are within reach as long as I stay focused.

WORK-LIFE BALANCE: DOES IT REALLY EXIST?

What book about a small business would be complete without the author saying something about work-life balance? And gee, talk about one of the key buzzwords of the decade. And you may be asking yourself the question—does work-life balance really exist?

Sure it does. But it's up to you to create it. Don't make the mistake— see what I did there?—of blaming your lack of work-life balance on something or someone else. If you feel overwhelmed, have too much on your plate, or have let your mental and physical health take a backseat, you are doing something wrong. And it is up to you to create change. No one can do that for you. Did you read that? Read it again. No one can create the change you need for your life but you.

Now that I have landed that message let me say this—I absolutely love what I do. I actually caught myself telling someone the other day about how much fun I had writing about dog poop for one of my clients. And it's true. It just so happens that for me, writing about dog poop and poop-scooping services is totally fun.

But I also get a lot of joy writing about most topics for my clients. I love writing about personal finance. I love talking about health and wellness. I love writing about the challenges that other small business owners, especially writers, face. So I am fortunate in that. However, that love for what I do can also put me in a place where I could be writing all the time. And I mean, all the time. I often have such a healthy backlog that I could write for ten or twelve hours, only to do it again the next day. And I'd probably be happy as a clam doing it.

The problem is that even when you love what you do, you need to step away sometimes. Just last night, I had planned to write this very chapter you are reading right now. But after a long day—it happened to be a Friday—and looking back at what I had accomplished for the week and my over-achievement of my revenue targets, I decided I should take a break. Rather, I needed a break.

So instead of writing all night, I took the night off. And it was the greatest gift I could give myself. I put on my comfy clothes, warmed up some dinner—it was one of our fend-for-yourself and heat-up leftover nights—and got cozy on the couch with the latest book I was reading. If you love to read, by the way, look me up and connect with me on Goodreads and Instagram. I am always posting about what I'm reading, my growing want-to-read list—I think I have a bookstore problem— and yadda, yadda, yadda.

But I digress. The point is that I gave myself the gift of time. I gave myself permission to walk away from my self-imposed deadline. I allowed myself a night off. And it was pure bliss.

And this morning? Instead of logging into my laptop right away to get started on this chapter, I headed off to a book signing at a local bookstore with one of my neighbors. And we had a blast! I met two authors. I bought all four of the books that were available at the event, and the authors signed each and every one. Then, my neighbor and I headed off down the street for lunch, did some shopping, and went to the bookstore that had hosted the event. I bought four more books. But who's counting?

Again, I digress. As you can tell, I love to read. I love, love, love books. My point in sharing this with you is to go back to that time management thing we discussed earlier and revisit what I had to say about boundaries and work-life balance. Set yourself up to experience these same moments—and hours—of joy, like I did. Doing so will be well worth it. You'll be a better person for your family. You'll be a better person for your clients. And you'll be a better person for you.

Take that hike you've been pushing off because you've been too busy. Take the family to the zoo. Schedule a date night with your special someone. Do what you love to do. And don't look back. Your business and your life will thank you for it.

BUILDING YOUR SUPPORT NETWORK

Let's end this chapter about turning your mistakes into mastery by talking about the importance of a support system. This is where a lot of writers can inadvertently get sucked down the rabbit hole of their introvertedness, forgetting about how humans thrive on relationships with other humans. And trust me, as an extroverted introvert, I get it. People exhaust me. I am perfectly happy to stay at home day in and day out and just do my thing.

But that's not always a good thing, especially if you are a writer like me that doesn't require a lot of day-to-day client interaction. You can get so focused on your work that you forget to take time to interact with people. And while reclusiveness works for some, I don't encourage it if you want to manage a successful copywriting business.

So, who is your support system? And if you don't have one today, how do you build one? These are great questions, and they don't always come with easy answers. I'll attempt to guide you here, but before I do, let me give you some context on my support system and network.

I'm fortunate to have some great friend groups that like to get together several times throughout the year. This allows me to get out, go out, and interact. I come home from those events drained but with a feeling of contentment that I didn't necessarily have before I left for the event.

For business owners, your support system may need to extend beyond your closest family members and friends. Remember, these people love you. They think you are awesome. They may even think you can do no wrong. They're the first to buy your books when they hit bookstore shelves. They're the first ones to share your social media posts. And that's all good stuff. But it isn't the support system you need to help you grow and scale your business.

You need a professional support system beyond just cheerleaders. This is where building relationships with people who won't just tell you what you want to hear becomes really important. You want a support network filled with individuals who will push you, challenge you, and even play devil's advocate with you at times. These people will help you see things from a different angle and grow your business in ways you might not have thought about on your own.

Here are a few pointers for growing that professional support system:

- **Seek out mentors or peers who challenge you.** Look for people who will give you honest feedback, even if it's uncomfortable. These are the folks who aren't afraid to tell you when your idea could use a little more work—or when you're playing it too safe.

- **Network outside your industry.** It's easy to surround yourself with like-minded people who think the way you do. But sometimes, the best advice comes from those outside your usual circles. They bring fresh perspectives that can inspire new ideas.

- **Join professional groups or associations.** Whether it's online or in-person, joining a group of like-minded business owners or writers can be a great way to expand your network. Don't just join for the sake of being there, though—get involved. Attend events, contribute to discussions, and build relationships.

- **Find accountability partners.** Partner with someone who can hold you accountable for your goals, deadlines, and growth. An accountability partner helps keep you on track and can offer a different viewpoint on issues you're dealing with.

- **Look for those who are where you want to be.** Surround yourself with people who have already achieved the kind of success you're aiming for. They've been through the trenches and can give you the guidance you need to avoid common pitfalls. Remember that book event I went to this morning? Besides the fact that I love to read, this was one of the very reasons I wanted to attend. I wanted to hear their advice for me when I started my next book.

Remember, the goal is to surround yourself with people who will help you improve—not just those who will tell you what you want to hear. Building this kind of network takes time and effort, but it's worth it in the long run.

YOU'RE ALWAYS LEARNING

Okay, I was just kidding when I said the last section would help us wrap up this chapter. But I have some more to say. Remember that no matter how great you are as a copywriter, content creator, author, or whatever, you are not, and you will never be, perfect. Embrace this! It permits you to keep making mistakes. More importantly, it lets you keep learning.

I've already told you that I see myself as a lifelong learner, and I can't emphasize this enough. As a writer, I get to learn something new every day. Whether I am looking up some statistics or facts to weave into a piece for one of my clients or making a mistake and figuring out what to do next, these are learning opportunities. It requires keeping an open mind to embrace feedback, grow, and get even better at what you do.

This doesn't always mean never following your gut, however. No one knows you like you do. So if you believe in something, see it through. What's the harm? You screw up? The way I see it, that mishap is a gift. Because now you know. And once you know, you know, right?

Learning never stops, and that's a beautiful thing. We're all just winging it half the time, and that's okay. It's part of the journey. Mistakes aren't something to be afraid of; they're actually little badges of honor. Every time you make one, it's a sign you're out there, giving it your best shot. And that's way better than sitting on the sidelines.

In fact, this leads me perfectly into our next chapter: "Mistakes Are Proof That You Are Trying." Because let's face it, the only people who never make mistakes are the ones who aren't doing anything at all. Let's dig into why messing up is actually a sign of progress—and how you can turn those flops into fuel to help your business and you be the best that they can be.

NOTES

MISTAKES ARE PROOF
THAT YOU ARE TRYING

NOT ALL THAT LONG AGO, my stepdaughter brought home a picture from school that she and her dad hung on the refrigerator in our kitchen. I practically stopped in my tracks when I saw it, not necessarily because I loved her incorporation of color—though she does do an amazing job of bringing color, energy, and emotion into all of her pictures—but because of what the picture had to say.

Mistakes are proof that you are trying.

I found this message particularly interesting and wildly coincidental, if not uncanny, as I was in the final stages of writing this book at that time. A book all about mistakes. A book all about giving it your best and not letting those mistakes stop you or get you down.

And she brings home this message. It was powerful, to say the least.

Though this chapter was not part of my initial plan, I extended my own writing deadline to add it. This message has so much to say in its seven short words that I felt we needed to talk about it a bit.

I know that many of you reading this book are still afraid to get off the couch and try. Whether it's starting that blog you've been thinking about for months, pitching your services to potential clients, or even just updating your LinkedIn profile (yes, I know it's a bit dusty), you might be holding back.

Maybe you're afraid of getting rejected, or that no one will read what you have to say. Or maybe it's the fear of messing up, like sending a client the wrong draft or posting something that doesn't get a single like. Trust me, I've been there.

But here's the thing: Staying on the sidelines because you're afraid to fail is the real mistake. Because mistakes are just proof that you're actually doing something. You're trying. And that's where growth happens.

I know what you're thinking—Ann, that's all well and good, but I just don't know how to get started. Here's my counter to that: Is there really only one right way to start doing what you want to do? Is there only one path forward? Of course not! And if you get it wrong the first time? Try, try again.

So, let's brainstorm—okay, I'll brainstorm and you can think through these ideas for yourself—on all those little mistakes you might make when you start trying. These aren't the top ten mistakes I talked about earlier in this book. These are those little mistakes that, even though small, can make you smack your forehead wondering what the heck happened. But I'll ask you this—are they really mistakes? Or are they simply stepping stones?

Let's think through it. And let's have some fun with it along the way.

BLUNDER # 1: OVERLOADING ON FREE ADVICE

Okay, your job is not to be the free and endless giver of advice to your clients. You know your stuff, and you deserve to be compensated for the work that you are doing. If you were in a corporate environment, you would be paid for the time that you spent putting together proposals, countless decks with recommendations, and so on. So why shouldn't you be compensated for your time spent in the freelance space?

This doesn't mean you can't offer free advice from time to time. But you do need to build some parameters so that you don't create a precedent that your clients will expect to get going forward.

Overloading on free advice is a big mistake because it sets an expectation that your expertise doesn't have value. Once you start giving away too much, it becomes harder to set boundaries later. To get over this without slowing your momentum, establish clear guidelines for what's free and what requires payment.

Offer a taste of your expertise, but make it clear that the real value lies in the paid services you provide. By doing this, you not only protect your time, but also maintain the respect of your clients—and your own sense of worth.

BLUNDER # 2: SAYING "YES" TO EVERYTHING

It can be so easy to say yes to anything and everything, especially when your business is first getting started. And while I encourage you to take on some small projects, even a handful at a lower rate to help you get some testimonials, reviews, and completed work under your belt, you need to manage expectations from the get-go.

So, here is my advice. Say yes strategically. It's okay to take on smaller projects or ones that might not pay top dollar in the beginning, but make sure you're clear about your boundaries—whether it's in terms of time, revisions, or the scope of work. You don't want to overcommit and burn yourself out before your business has even taken off. Learn to evaluate each opportunity and ask yourself if it aligns with your long-term goals before saying yes.

BLUNDER # 3: CREATING A TO-DO LIST THAT'S WAY TOO AMBITIOUS

Remember that whole chapter about turning your mistakes into mastery and allowing yourself some work-life balance? If you find yourself with a to-do list that's way too long, you might want to revisit that section. I know that there's a lot to do when getting your business underway.

You need to build a website, set up your social media profiles, research your target audience, design a logo, file your business with the state, create business cards, draft contracts, organize your taxes, update your LinkedIn, write blog posts, send emails, follow up on emails, make sure your invoicing system works, and, oh yeah, actually do the client work that's supposed to pay your bills.

It's easy to feel like "trying" means "doing everything right this second," but that's a recipe for burnout. The reality is some things can wait. Focus on what moves the needle first, and tackle the rest little by little. No one's handing out awards for the longest to-do list!

BLUNDER # 4: UNDERPRICING YOUR FIRST CLIENT PROJECT

I know I had an entire chapter focused on rate cards and not undervaluing your services. But, this is really about that first project. Figuring out the right price can be a bit of a conundrum. You want to price it low enough that the client will bite and you can get that experience, but you don't want to price it so low that you give that client the reputation that you are a "cheap" writer. And remember, cheap and affordable are two very different things.

So, how do you find that sweet spot for your first project? Start by doing a little market research—check what other beginner writers in your niche are charging, and go for somewhere in that range. Remember, you're pricing for experience at this stage, not perfection. It's okay to price a little lower to get your foot in the door, but make sure it still reflects the value you're bringing. And don't forget to set clear expectations with the client—whether it's the number of revisions or the project scope—so they understand they're getting a great deal without thinking you're always going to be their budget writer.

BUDGET # 5: MISJUDGING HOW LONG A PROJECT WILL TAKE

Oh, this is such a fun challenge, even after years in the business. How long will a project take? Let me add some color to this one. I love it when clients want a time estimate, especially those who you are charging your hourly rate. How are you supposed to know how long it will take?

Say you have an editing project that you are working on and the client says that they have 10,000 words for you to edit and want an estimate. Umm, how should you know? Obviously, something well-written and already run through editing tools will be far easier to edit than something that hasn't been looked over. And it's really the same with writing.

What you need to do here is manage client expectations and also manage your time really, really well. To figure out how long it takes you to write, you need to write. So, if you don't have an initial fixed-rate project to work on, you need to come up with one on your own.

To get a sense of how long it takes you to write, start by choosing some moderately challenging topics—something you're familiar with but don't know everything about. Then, write 1,000 words on it. Pay close attention to how long it takes you to research, organize your thoughts, and actually put fingers to keyboard. This will give you a solid idea of your writing speed and help you estimate more accurately for future projects. It's a bit of trial and error, but it's the best way to understand your workflow—and trust me, your clients will appreciate a more realistic estimate.

BLUNDER # 6: SENDING AN EMAIL WITHOUT DOUBLE CHECKING WHO IT'S TO

I totally had to add this to the list of blunders. We've all done it at some point in our careers. And, oh, how embarrassing this can be. For example, I have two gentlemen named Matt with whom I work regularly. And it just so happens that their last names start with the same letter. I am always sending them the wrong emails. While I blame Gmail for popping in the wrong name, this is my fault and my responsibility alone. But it happens.

Here's what I'll tell you. First, remember that your emails are an electronic record. You may think you're deleting an email, but it never really disappears. So, follow some basic email etiquette: Never air your dirty laundry in an email, never disparage someone—especially a client—and never share something confidential without clearly marking it as such. Add the appropriate encryption if necessary, and always double, triple, and quadruple-check that you've got the right recipient.

And speaking of recipients, can I mention my pet peeve about names? Always, always, always check the spelling of the first and last name. I can't tell you how many emails I've received addressed to Anne or Amy when my name is right there. It feels careless, and clients will feel the same way if you get their name wrong. So don't let it happen!

BLUNDER # 7: SENDING THE EMAIL WITHOUT THE ATTACHMENT

You may be wondering why I added this one. Well, when sending and receiving client deliverables, this is more important than you might realize. Missing a deadline because you forgot an attachment is not only embarrassing but bad for your business.

So, how do you avoid this all-too-common blunder? A simple tip: Before you hit send, make it a habit to check for attachments when writing emails that require them. Many email platforms even prompt you when you mention an attachment but don't include one—pay attention to those reminders. And remember, missing an attachment can be a sign that you're moving too fast. Slow down, breathe, and review the email carefully to make sure everything is in place before you send it off.

If you forget the attachment and don't notice for a day or two, you're the one accountable, not the client. But hey, mistakes like this? They're proof that you're trying. Just make sure to learn from it and move forward a little more carefully next time.

BLUNDER # 8: NOT READING THE CONTRACT CAREFULLY

I've already talked ad nauseam about MSAs and SOWs. And, when you are the one sending the contract, you should be intimately familiar with what the contract contains. But sometimes, a client will redline—a.k.a. edit—the contact ferociously. Or they will ask to work with their own paper because much of the content has already been reviewed, agreed on, and approved by their legal team.

These situations are okay, but you need to ask yourself two questions before you move forward:

- Is the client relationship worth the extra effort to review?
- Is the cost of having an attorney review the new contract or redlining something you can afford and still come out profitable on the other side?

I haven't been in a situation to turn down a client because of their contract. Nor have I had a client provide a lengthy list of redlines. And I believe that is for two reasons. First, I invested a healthy budget into having my contracts created by a reliable and reputable attorney. Second, my contract terms are simple. I do the work, you pay me for the work, you own the work. You don't pay me for the work, you don't own the work. Pretty simple, right?

This all said, if you get into the position of working off your client's legal paper instead of your own, look for these items that can get you into trouble if you don't know what you are signing up for.

First, check the payment terms carefully. You don't want to find out after the fact that the client's standard is 90-day payment terms when you were expecting 30 days. You're a small business. You might not be able to afford to wait for payment for 90 days. Pay close attention to your cash flow. Also, pay attention to the scope of work. Sometimes, clients sneak in extra tasks or responsibilities that weren't part of your original agreement. Finally, keep an eye on ownership rights—who owns the work once it's delivered? Make sure it's clear that you retain ownership until payment is received.

If something looks off, don't be afraid to ask questions or push back. Contracts aren't just formalities—they define your working relationship, so it's worth taking the time to understand them fully before you sign. Better to catch issues now than be stuck in a bad deal later.

BLUNDER #9: OVERLOADING ON TOOLS AND SOFTWARE

Oh, the excitement of finding that perfect tool to organize your life and your business! I totally get it—I'm still adding tools to my arsenal as I go. But here's the thing: You don't need to sign up for every project management tool, time tracker, and writing app all at once. In fact, that can actually slow you down. You'll spend more time managing your tools than getting any real work done.

Start small. Pick one or two tools that meet your immediate needs, and get comfortable with them before adding more. Trust me, you don't need ten apps that all do the same thing. Keep it simple, or you'll end up spending more time learning how to use your tools than actually using them to move your business forward.

Want to know the tools I use each day? Grammarly, Copyscape, Originality.AI, ChatGPT 4.0 (for outlines and idea generation), and Headline Studio. They keep my workflow smooth and my projects on track without overcomplicating things. If you need a place to start, start there.

BLUNDER # 10: SUBMITTING WITHOUT PROOFREADING

Ouch. You did what you never should have done. You sent work to a client and you didn't proofread it first. Yikes. But, let yourself off the hook a bit. We've all done it. We're in a hurry. Too many things on our plate. You and Grammarly or the Hemingway App aren't getting along. Yes, it happens.

And while this is a big one, don't let it get you down. Own up to your mistake. Fix the errors. And get back to it. What's the worst thing that can happen? The client doesn't rehire you? You'll find another. Sure, that client was important. You don't want to lose them. You didn't want to lose them. But the time you spend sulking and being mad at yourself is just taking up too much valuable real estate in that writing mind of yours.

Like I said, the best way to handle this is to apologize to the client right away. Acknowledge the mistake, offer a quick and clean fix, and don't make excuses. Something simple like, "I realize there were some errors in the document I sent, and I've corrected them here. Thank you for your understanding" goes a long way.

Clients appreciate honesty and accountability, and showing that you're willing to take responsibility and fix the issue can actually build trust. Moving forward, slow down, prioritize proofreading, and use a checklist to prevent this blunder from happening again.

BLUNDER # 11: NOT CONTRIBUTING TO A 401(K)

This one is big enough that it could have easily been listed as one of the top ten mistakes I made in my first year as a copywriter. But thankfully, it wasn't something I forgot to do. Having worked in the finance space for the greater part of my career, and since I got my professional writing start in the personal finance space, this was top of mind for me. But it might not be top of mind for you.

So, I am going to end my list of blunders with this one. Even if you are self-employed, you can contribute to a 401(k). Though the amount tends to change year over year, at the time I wrote this book, you could contribute up to $69,000 to a self-employment 401(k). And you can contribute up to $7,000 to a Roth IRA.

Sure, you might not have the benefit of employer matches or contributions, but retirement planning should always be on your mind as someone in the self-employment space. And getting started is easy. Reach out to a personal finance or investment expert near you or ask friends or family members for some recommendations. It only takes a few signatures and a few days to get started. Avoid putting this off. Before you know it, you can be two years into your business without a growing retirement account.

BOUNCING BACK AFTER MISTAKES AND BLUNDERS

Bouncing back after a mistake can feel challenging, but doing so doesn't have to be. It just means you have to embrace a learning mindset and a willingness to try, try again.

To end this chapter, I'll leave you with some tips on what works best for me when I am frustrated with a mistake I have made or come across one of those "why didn't I think of that" moments.

- **Sleep on it.** Sometimes, a good night's sleep is all you need to put things in perspective. Let your brain hit the reset button, and you'll often wake up with fresh ideas or solutions to the problem.

- **Curl up with your favorite book.** Take a step back from the situation. Grab that book you've been meaning to finish and let your worries float away for a bit. A little relaxation can do wonders for your creativity.

- **Get outside and move.** Whether it's a quick walk around the block or a long hike, getting some fresh air and movement can clear your head and help you bounce back with renewed energy.

- **Write it out.** Sometimes just writing down your frustrations can help you let go of them. Free-write for five minutes about the mistake you made—don't hold back! Once it's out on paper, it tends to lose its grip on you.

- **Laugh it off.** Humor really is a great way to break the tension. Call a friend who makes you laugh or watch a silly video. Laughing at your mistake helps you take yourself less seriously and bounce back faster.

- **Shift focus to something else.** If you're hitting a wall, shift gears. Work on a different project or a task you enjoy. Sometimes, a mental break from the problem helps bring fresh ideas later.

- **Remind yourself of past wins.** Look back at how far you've come and remind yourself of all the successes you've had. Everyone makes mistakes, but you've also had plenty of victories. Let those boost your confidence to keep going.

- **Have a spontaneous dance party.** Just kidding! You'll never catch me dancing around the house, and if you're like me, this one probably isn't happening. But hey, I wanted to see if you were still reading! If the thought of busting out some moves makes you cringe, feel free to skip this tip. But if dancing's your thing, go ahead and twirl around the living room—just make sure the curtains are closed, unless you are into that sort of a thing. And that's a book for another day by a different author.

My message to you is that mistakes are inevitable, but how you recover is what really counts.

NOTES

LOOKING FORWARD:

MY SECOND YEAR (AND BEYOND) AS A COPYWRITER

ONE OF THE THINGS I TALK ABOUT in a lot of the content I write for clients is business continuity and forward-thinking. And when I say business continuity, I am not talking about disaster planning. I'm talking about how you can keep your business new and fresh.

We've all read the horror stories of businesses that failed to innovate and are no longer around. And there were some pretty big companies that, just a few decades ago, we could never have imagined folding simply because they didn't keep up with customer demands. But the fact is that's exactly what happened to companies such as Blockbuster and Kodak. These were giants in their industries—household names that seemed unstoppable. I mean, don't you remember those weekend trips to Blockbuster to pick up some VHS tapes, and, later, DVDs? Okay, perhaps I just dated myself, but trust me, this was a thing.

Yet, companies like the two I mentioned are perfect examples of what happens when a business fails to innovate or keep up with changing customer demands. Blockbuster didn't adapt to the rise of streaming services like Netflix, and Kodak hesitated to embrace the digital photography revolution. Both had opportunities to pivot but stayed stuck in their old ways, believing their existing models would carry them through.

It's a tough reminder that no matter how successful you are, resting on your laurels isn't an option. Whether you're a multi-billion dollar company or a solo copywriter, you need to evolve to stay relevant. Customer needs change, new technology emerges, and trends come and go. If you're not paying attention to what's next, you risk becoming the next cautionary tale in business failure.

So what does this mean for a copywriter or content writer who spends their time writing for other clients? Sure, it means hoping that those businesses will continue to innovate so that you can continue to deliver a steady stream of great content for their website and marketing needs. But what about your business? You need to be innovating, too.

To be honest, this is the type of thing that keeps me up at night. And if you are just getting started with your business, it may be keeping you up too. Just how do we, as content creators for others, focus on keeping our business front and center and in high demand?

Here are a few things that I have been working on.

In the spring of 2024, I started a vlog—a.k.a. a video blog—as a way to not only talk about my own books but also share insights on the books I'm reading and key business takeaways from the Copywriting For You blog. (Which, by the way, if you aren't yet subscribed to my YouTube channel, stop reading and go subscribe now. You can find me at https://www.youtube.com/@CopywritingForYou. I'll wait. And once you've subscribed and watched a couple of videos, come back and keep reading. I promise this will still be here when you return!)

So, when we think about innovation and keeping up with customers and their changing needs, it only made sense for me to create a video channel. Vlogs have become such a big thing. Video content is engaging, personal, and creates a real connection with your audience. For copywriters like us, starting a vlog can be a great way to share your personality and expertise while reaching new potential clients.

It's not just about writing anymore—it's about showing people who you are, and a vlog is a great way to do that. Whether you're talking about writing tips, behind-the-scenes looks at your process, or even giving updates on your favorite reads, vlogs can open doors to more visibility and opportunities.

I've also renewed my focus on social media, which we discussed earlier. After a slow start, I've been trying to post more often with relevant content that feels authentic to me. One of my favorite parts of this renewed effort has been discovering 'Bookstagrammers'—people who love talking about books as much as I do.

After a five-year hiatus from reading (not entirely by choice, but due to life circumstances that made reading a challenge for my mental health), I'm finally back at it. Now, I have quite the stack of books on my want-to-read list. The Bookstagram community has been a great source of inspiration and connection for me, and it's such a fun way to mix business with personal passion.

Plus, it seems that the more I read, the better my writing seems to get. Ask me how reading the latest love story, mystery, or thriller helps me become a better personal finance or health and wellness writer and I'll likely look at you like a deer in the headlights. But go with me on this one. The more I read, the easier the words flow, the more productive I am, and the more I enjoy what I do because I am taking the time I need and deserve for self-care. It just so happens that my favorite past-time aside from spending time with my family is reading—and buying—books.

Speaking of books, let's not forget that I'm now writing my own! My first book, *Perseverance. Reinvention.*, was self-published in June 2024 and will be re-released by Fox Pointe Publishing at the end of 2024. And this book you're reading now? It's coming out in early 2025! So if you have it, we're probably somewhere in 2025 or beyond at this point.

Writing has become such a big part of my life, and it's exciting to think about what's next. I've got two more books in the very early planning phases, and while I can't reveal too much just yet, I can promise they'll continue to explore the themes of creativity, perseverance, and finding your path.

But that's just me. What if becoming a published author is not as exciting of an idea for you as it is for me? What if starting a vlog is not your thing? That's okay. It just means that you need to be creative and come up with your own ideas, especially as you enter your second, third, fourth—you get the picture—year of writing.

Here are some things you might want to consider.

Let's start with the low-hanging fruit—small, manageable changes that can make a big difference in your copywriting business. One of the easiest ways to innovate is by expanding the types of content you offer. If you've been mainly writing blog posts or web copy, why not try your hand at email marketing or social media campaigns?

Email newsletters are still one of the most effective ways for businesses to connect with their audience, and writing persuasive, engaging emails is a skill that's always in demand. The best part? You can test the waters with one or two clients before deciding if it's something you want to offer long-term.

Learning new tools or platforms is another great way to keep things fresh. Maybe vlogging isn't for you, but what about creating a content portfolio using platforms like Behance or Dribbble? These platforms are designed for creative professionals to share their work in a way that looks great, which can set you apart from the traditional website portfolio. Plus, having a portfolio on a specialized platform can help potential clients find you more easily. Think of this as a way to go above and beyond what Upwork or Fiverr has to offer.

Now, for something a bit more outside the box: offer workshops or one-on-one training. As copywriters, we sometimes forget that what comes naturally to us—writing, crafting compelling headlines, understanding tone and voice—doesn't come as easily to others. Think about offering workshops or short training sessions to business owners or marketing teams who need help with content strategy or writing basics. Not only is this a great way to share your expertise, but it's also a fantastic way to build relationships and potentially gain long-term clients. Remember how I talked about building that support network? Well, here's a great way to add to it.

If teaching isn't your thing, diversifying the industries you write for is another way to innovate. Sometimes we get comfortable writing for the same types of businesses, whether it's health and wellness, tech, or finance. While having a niche is great, stepping into new industries can broaden your skills and client base. Not sure where to start? Consider industries you've always been curious about or those that are currently trending. Research a bit, offer to write a test piece, and see if it sparks new creativity.

Now, let's move to some of the bigger rocks you can tackle to take your business to the next level. One major idea is partnering with complementary service providers, like graphic designers or SEO experts. By bundling your copywriting services with theirs, you can offer more value to clients and expand your service offerings without having to learn a whole new skill set yourself. It's a win-win. You get to focus on what you do best—writing—while also providing clients with a full-service package.

You might also consider creating a course or ebook around your copywriting expertise. Sounds like a great idea—I should do that. No, this doesn't mean becoming a full-time educator, but sharing what you know in a structured format can position you as an authority in your field. Courses can be pre-recorded and sold passively, which means you're adding another revenue stream to your business without constant upkeep. It's also a great way to reach a broader audience and maybe even connect with future clients who wouldn't have otherwise found you.

You can also think about collaborating with other writers or content creators. It doesn't have to be formal, but partnering with others in your industry can lead to new opportunities and ideas. Whether it's guest writing on each other's blogs or working together on a joint project, collaborating can help you learn from others, expand your reach, and keep your business growing in unexpected ways.

Plus, there's an added SEO benefit: backlinks. For those new to the SEO thing, a backlink is simply a link on someone else's website that leads back to your site. Think of it as a vote of confidence—their site is essentially saying, "Hey, check this out, it's worth your time." Backlinks are especially valuable when they come from websites with high domain authority (a measure of how credible and trusted a site is in the eyes of search engines). A do-follow link is a specific kind of backlink that tells search engines to count that link as a positive signal for your site, which can help improve your search rankings.

The key here is to keep experimenting, learning, and evolving. What works for one person may not work for you, and that's okay. The most important thing is that you're trying new things, making mistakes, and finding what keeps your business moving forward. After all, if Blockbuster and Kodak had taken that same approach, they might still be around today.

THE EMOTIONAL PART OF FREELANCING

As I get close to calling this book a wrap, there are a few more points I want to share with you that can hopefully help your business be the best it can be. Short of stealing taglines from other companies, let's talk for a moment about the emotional side of freelancing.

Getting started with your own business is a big decision. It doesn't have to be a hard one, and the steps are actually not all that complicated when you boil it down, but it's a big decision nonetheless. And it can be an emotional one, too. It's especially emotional when your deliverable is quite literally the words that you write. Your words are a part of you. Even when you are writing for someone else, they are your words, and you are allowing someone else to take credit. That can be a lot to comprehend and manage at first.

Then the imposter syndrome creeps in, making you wonder if you're really cut out for this freelance life. Or the fear of rejection when a client passes on your proposal or doesn't like your first draft. I've been there, too. And let's not forget the dreaded dry spell when it feels like everyone is ghosting you—or you stopped focusing on lead generation—and suddenly your inbox is emptier than you'd like. It's easy to let doubt sink in.

But here's the thing, every single freelancer goes through this. The emotional highs and lows are part of the journey. Building a support system can make all the difference. Whether it's joining online writing communities, forming a mastermind group, or simply reaching out to fellow freelancers for a chat, having people to lean on helps manage the rollercoaster. You don't have to do this alone. And trust me, the highs—when a client raves about your work or when you land that dream project—are worth every low.

BALANCING YOUR CREATIVE SIDE WITH YOUR BUSINESS MIND

Another thing that can be challenging for new copywriters and content writers is the balance between being a creative and needing to manage a business. The creative side is likely why you got into the business, but you still need to manage the business.

And I hate to throw a scary statistic out there to you, but over 80% of businesses fail because of cash flow. And that means that they're not managing the business side well. They're either undercharging, not invoicing in a timely manner, not following up on overdue payments, or worse, they didn't put a contract in place and now have no legal recourse to get paid for their work. Ouch.

Balancing your creative side and desire for the work is simply something you need to balance with managing the business. So please make sure you have a plan in place to protect yourself and your income. That means setting clear payment terms, creating contracts that outline your expectations, and making invoicing a priority.

You might love writing, but if you're not getting paid, that passion can quickly turn to frustration. It's important to schedule time for the "business" side of freelancing, whether that's checking in on invoices, filing taxes, or managing cash flow. The creative work is fun, but keeping your business running smoothly is what allows you to keep doing it.

DEVELOPING YOUR PERSONAL BRAND

As a small business owner getting out into the world to promote and sell your content writing services, you are putting your name out there. And your name is your brand. Let's look at my company as an example. My company name is Copywriting For You. But anyone who hires me knows quite quickly that they are actually hiring Ann Schreiber.

If they have a great experience, they had a great experience with Ann Schreiber. If they had a bad experience, well, you get the idea. And so you need to keep this front and center in all of your business interactions and whenever and wherever you are representing your business.

Developing your personal brand is so important as a freelance writer because you are your business. Your name, your work ethic, and your style are all part of the package you're offering to clients. Personal branding helps you stand out in a crowded field. It's what makes potential clients say, "I want to work with you specifically." To create a strong personal brand, start by developing a unique voice. What makes your writing different? What's your approach to client work? Defining your niche also helps. Whether you specialize in health and wellness, finance, or tech, being clear about what you're great at makes you more attractive to the right clients.

Make sure your online presence—your website, social media, and even your email signature—reflects this brand. Everything should tell the story of who you are and what you offer, so potential clients can easily see how you'll fit their needs.

SETTING AND MEETING YOUR LONG-TERM GOALS

Last but not least, keep your eye on the prize, whatever that particular prize might be for you. Perhaps you have an income goal. Maybe you want to get a published byline somewhere—I remember when I first started to get bylines and it was such an exciting and overwhelming experience—or maybe you, too, want to write your first book.

Whatever your goals are, make it part of your business to put in place the steps you need to take to meet those goals. Start by breaking them down into smaller, actionable tasks. For example, if your goal is to increase your income, set a specific target and determine how many clients or projects you'll need to reach it. If your dream is to get published, make a list of publications you want to pitch and set aside time each week to focus on submissions.

Goals like writing your first book might seem overwhelming, but they become achievable when you chip away at them bit by bit. Set a word count target for each week and, before you know it, you'll have your first draft.

Maybe your goal is just to become an amazing copywriter and keep typing away. That's okay too as long as you remember to keep up with the times. Remember, meeting your goals is about consistent effort and small wins along the way.

Celebrate each milestone, and keep moving forward.

WHAT'S NEXT?

Before I get into what's next for me—something I just briefly mentioned earlier in this chapter—let's recap some of what we've talked about in this book and why I wrote it in the first place.

This book isn't just about my top ten mistakes as a new copywriter; it's about how those mistakes shaped me, my business, and my journey as a writer. As I mentioned earlier, these aren't the only mistakes I've made (far from it!), but they are the big ones—the ones that gave me a roadmap for improvement.

I wrote this book to help you, fellow writers and small business owners, not make the same stumbles. Sure, you'll still make mistakes (we all do!), but hopefully, you can skip a few of the forehead-smacking moments I encountered along the way.

To recap, here are the ten key mistakes we discussed:

- **Going Cheap and Getting a Poorly Designed Website:** Trying to save money on a website ended up costing me more in time, frustration, and lost opportunities. Your website is your storefront—invest in it.

- **Not Having Clients Sign a Statement of Work:** Verbal agreements don't cut it. You need everything in writing—clear, detailed, and signed—before starting any work.

- **Missteps in Pricing—The Cost of Undervaluing My Services:** Underpricing your work not only undervalues your skills but also sets a precedent that's hard to break. Know your worth and charge for it.

- **Not Spending Enough Time on Lead Generation:** Expecting clients to find you isn't a strategy. I learned the hard way that lead generation needs to be a constant focus.

- **Not Looking Out for My Business with Liability Insurance:** The "it won't happen to me" mindset is dangerous. Protect yourself with proper business insurance—because things can happen.

- **Waiting Too Long to Leverage Social Media:** I sat on the sidelines of social media far too long. It's one of the easiest, most affordable ways to get your name out there and connect with potential clients.

- **Not Posting Regular Content to My Blog:** Building a blog is just the first step. Regular, consistent content is what keeps your audience engaged and your SEO strong.

- **Relying Too Much (or Not Enough) on Artificial Intelligence:** Finding the right balance with AI tools can be tricky, but it's essential. AI can save time, but it can't replace your unique voice or creativity.

- **Failing to Develop Business Partnerships:** Trying to go it alone doesn't always work. Building partnerships with complementary service providers can open doors and grow your business.

- **Not Starting My Business Sooner:** The biggest regret? Not starting sooner. Don't wait for the perfect moment—it doesn't exist. Jump in, make mistakes, and learn along the way.

By sharing these, my goal is simple: I want to help you get off to the races faster than I did. Avoid the potholes I hit, and focus on growing your business from day one. I made these mistakes so you don't have to! Now, let's talk about what's next for me and for you.

For me, I'm about to shut down my laptop, hug it to my chest, and let myself celebrate the completion of my second book. While the hard work is just beginning—the editing, the cover design, the publishing—I look forward to working with Fox Pointe Publishing and seeing where this book will go.

And tomorrow, who knows what's next? Maybe I'll start writing that next book. To be honest, the future is bright, and I have many ideas. It's just time to get those next ideas onto paper.

And for you? The world is your oyster.

ACKNOWLEDGMENTS

WHERE DO YOU REALLY BEGIN when you want to thank everyone who helped you get to where you are today? It's almost like going on stage to receive an award, hoping against hope that you don't leave out anyone important. Talk about stress!

And here's the thing. I have so many people to thank. I have been so fortunate to meet and get to know hundreds of people throughout my life, all of whom have had some sort of impact that helped me become who I am. And so I apologize right now if I miss calling you out here. Please know that I am thankful for the role that you played and for being a presence in my life.

To that end, I have to start by thanking my family, especially my husband, Scott, whom I love with all my heart. I am so proud to be your wife, and I am glad to have you by my side. Thank you for your sense of humor and for everything you do to create a wonderful home for us to live and work in. And thank you for being the husband who supports a wife in all of her crazy writing—and reading—endeavors. I'm sure it's not always easy.

To my children, Cate and Zach, wow, I could not be prouder of you two. Cate, you have the biggest and most loving heart of anyone I have ever met. Some days I really wonder how and why God decided to bless me with you. You amaze me each and every day, and I am so blessed to be your mom. Zach, we have been through so much together. You have been so much more than a son. You have been my confidante and you were the one by my side as we picked up the pieces of our lives so many years ago. Thank you for being you.

To my son-in-law, Nathan, thank you for being my daughter's number one fan. Thank you for loving her, respecting her, and being her best friend in life. Knowing you have her back and are there for her every day makes my days just a little bit easier.

To my stepdaughter, Faith, you are the little one I choose to love, though you sure do make it easy. I give you a huge piece of my heart. Thank you for being you and for loving me as that bonus person in your life.

To my mom, dad, and sister. Thank you for the childhood you provided and all the life experiences you gave to me along the way. I am so fortunate to have grown up in our family, with every joy and challenge that came to us along the journey.

To my best friend, Kirsten, wow. You are and continue to be my best person. I love you tremendously. Your support and friendship through the thick and thin of it all deserves an award in and of itself. You are amazing and I am so grateful for your support and encouragement. And of course, thank you for all those hours of reading and editing my work.

To the Classy B's. I've thanked you before and I thank you again. How can one woman get so lucky to have a dozen or so friends there for her whenever she needs it? I only hope that I am as good a friend to all of you as you have been to me.

To Missy, Shelley, Jackie, Julie, Erin, Robin, Karen, and all those other ladies who tolerate me clicking away on my keyboard writing instead of crafting on our weekend getaways, thank you. I so enjoy our weekends away, gossiping about life and catching up on everyone's families.

To my neighbors, thank you for welcoming me into this neighborhood when Scott and me were first creating this life together. Thank you for being there for those walks, for those wine nights, and even for a good cry here and there. I am so fortunate to have found you and to have you all so close by.

To my new family, the Schreibers, thank you for welcoming me and my children into your lives. Thank you for supporting Scott and I as we have created this new life together. And thank you for supporting my writing journey and reading my books!

Last but so very not least, thank you to the team at Fox Pointe Publishing. Thank you for helping me take the jump from a self-published author to one with a team here to support me every step of the way. Kiersten, thank you for your leadership and guidance, and most importantly, your belief in me and helping me share my thoughts with the world. To Scotty, thank you for designing the most amazing book covers that help reflect who I am and the stories I have to tell. And to Emma, thank you for having my back and cleaning up my story in a way that makes me proud. I am so thankful to have all of you on my team.

GLOSSARY OF TERMS

I KNOW THIS BOOK IS FULL OF MARKETING-SPEAK, and for that, I am truly sorry, kind of. The truth of the matter is that I am indeed a marketer. While these days I focus my time on content writing, I have spent nearly 30 years in the marketing space. All those years have come to serve me well as a freelance writer, ghostwriter, and now author.

That said, many of my readers might not understand all of the terms and acronyms I used in this book. So, I thought I would take the time to help explain some of these terms so you have a bit more insight into what I am talking about.

AI Most people these days have heard of AI—artificial intelligence— even if they are not in the content or business space. The truth is that AI is everywhere. AI refers to computer systems that can perform tasks typically requiring human intelligence, like language processing, image recognition, and decision-making.
AI operates through machine learning, where algorithms learn and improve from data patterns over time without being explicitly pro-grammed for every action. In content creation, AI can analyze trends, suggest keywords, even generate draft content—refer back to the chapter on this very topic.

However, while it's a powerful tool, AI is only as good as the data and objectives guiding it, so human oversight is super important for keeping results relevant and creative.

B2B In content writing, B2B stands for "business-to-business"—meaning that the target audience for these marketing materials isn't your everyday consumer but rather another business. B2B copy focuses on demonstrating value, expertise, and solutions that help businesses improve their own operations or services.

For example, a software company might need a case study written to show a potential client (another business) how their product increases productivity. In my past life as the head of corporate marketing for a business process management company, our content focused on creating case studies of how our company helped other businesses become more successful and efficient in their call center operations.

B2B content is about making complex solutions accessible, useful, and relevant to professionals in a specific industry.

B2C If B2B is all about businesses talking to other businesses, then B2C is "business-to-consumer"—directly reaching the everyday people who use the product or service. B2C content focuses on creating an emotional connection, simplifying complex ideas, and making products or services appealing and accessible to individuals.

Think of product descriptions, social media posts, or blog articles aimed at showing consumers why they need that cool new gadget or service in their lives. B2C is about speaking to people's wants and needs, not just their professional goals. To put this in perspective, when you see emails from companies like FICO or Experian about your credit health, they are engaging in B2C marketing.

CMO The CMO is the Chief Marketing Officer of an organization. Though not all companies have a chief-level marketing position, this is pretty commonplace in larger organizations. The CMO is responsible for crafting strategies that build the brand, reach the target audience, and support sales goals.

The CMO leads other roles that you might be more familiar with, like the content marketing team, social media managers, and public relations (PR) specialists. The goal of the CMO is to make sure all efforts align with the big-picture strategy. The CMO's approach directly informs the content strategy by setting themes, messaging priorities, and goals that resonate with the audience, helping the content team understand what to create and why it matters to the brand's growth.

As a content writer, you won't likely take direction directly from the CMO. But you will likely be taking direction informed by the CMO.

MSA The MSA is the Master Services Agreement. This is an overarching document that outlines the high-level details of your working relationship with your clients. More specifically, it details payment terms, confidentiality, and intellectual property rights, so that everyone is on the same page.

The MSA is especially useful in long-term relationships, as it allows you to add specific project agreements in a Statement of Work (SOW) without renegotiating the basics each time. Trust me; you want an MSA to help prevent disagreements down the road.

SEO SEO stands for search engine optimization. While a book such as this doesn't need to worry about SEO, any content that is written for an online audience does. Search engine optimization is all about making online content visible to search engines like Google, so it reaches the right audience.

By optimizing content with relevant keywords, links, and a strong structure, writers help their work rank higher in search results. Good

SEO grows organic traffic, bringing more readers to the content naturally. It's a balance of pleasing both the algorithms (through keywords, metadata, and readability) and the audience, so they find content that's valuable, engaging, and easy to discover.

SOW I explained the MSA above, and the SOW (Statement of Work) is the next important part of those legal contracts that I discussed in the chapter about mistake # 2. An SOW represents the independent projects that you might do for a client. This document is tied to the MSA and covers individual projects' specifics, such as timelines, deliverables, costs, and any unique requirements. Each SOW is intended to keep both you and the client aligned on project-specific expectations. It's like a roadmap, setting clear goals and responsibilities for every new phase of work.

ABOUT THE AUTHOR

Ann Schreiber is an accomplished freelance copywriter, blogger, and owner of 'Copywriting For You.' She has been in the marketing and sales business for over 25 years and is passionate about business-focused writing.

She released her first book, *Perseverance. Reinvention*, in 2024. Her next book, *The Top 10 Mistakes I Made My First Year as a Copywriter*, will be released in the spring of 2025, which chronicles the mistakes she made during her first year as a small business owner in copywriting and content writing.

Ann received her bachelor's degree in English communications from the University of Minnesota and her master's degree in business communication from the University of St. Thomas. She has two adult children and remarried in February 2023. She is now blessed with a wonderful husband and young stepdaughter as well.

Ann enjoys reading when she isn't busy typing away on her laptop for her clients or for fun. Her favorite authors include Colleen Hoover, Jodi Picoult, and Kristin Hannah. Ann also enjoys spending time outdoors, working out on the Peloton, and taking her son's bassett hound for daily walks.